Awareness | Discovery | Wholen... | ...mation

THE HA...

Just as life is ... ...n recovery
are we faced ... ...y of hills to climb
and valleys to ... ...onstant is that we take
a searching look ... ...re we've been, where we are
now, and where we're going; our focus changes from
awareness of a problem, to discovery of solutions, to
the wholeness we can enjoy when solutions bring
peace, to the kinds of transformations that change us
at the deepest levels of our beings.

Awareness to *Discovery* to *Wholeness*, and *Transformation*.
The Recovery Horizon is Hazelden's commitment to
supporting you no matter where you are in your own
process of personal and spiritual growth.

AWARENESS

**Before recovery can truly start, we must
recognize our destructive behaviors or those
of someone we love. Only then can our real
work begin. We discover the Twelve Steps and
focus on them and their place in our lives, as
we take those first long looks at the factual
and clinical aspects of our problem.**

from "I Won't Wait Up Tonight"

Over the years, I've learned from the families who have come to the Hazelden Family Center how difficult it is to face up to problem drinking and drug abuse, to alcoholism and other drug addiction. I know about the fears and doubts you feel, your anger and frustration, your weariness, and your sheer despair. I've also seen your love and dedication. I've seen your patience, tolerance, and understanding. And I have seen your optimism in the face of problems that you can't seem to pin down and that you seem unable to do anything about.

And I've seen, although I really can't explain it, the wonderful and mysterious process that people go through when they regain self-confidence, find new directions for themselves, and eventually discover, looking back on it all, that managing to cope with this problem has enriched their lives. I want to pass on some of the things that I've learned from troubled families over the years, some things that you may find to be helpful.

Praise for "I Won't Wait Up Tonight"

"This book provides an abundance of important help to those living with the trauma and tragedy of chemical dependency."

> EARNIE LARSEN
> Author of *From Anger to Forgiveness*

"It is refreshing to read a book that describes families of alcoholics as intelligent, resourceful and resilient. Williams offers families new hope in his recognition that each family is unique and family members are capable of solving their problems once they become aware of their own natural resourcefulness."

> JOSEPH KELLERMANN
> Author of
> *Alcoholism: A Merry-Go-Round Named Denial*

"The miracle of this book is that Terence Williams writes about family resilience instead of dysfunction or codependence. What a breath of fresh air! He also describes family systems and their persisting patterns without using professional jargon. The Al-Anon message has never been written about with more eloquence and clarity. Everyone should read this book."

> PAULINE BOSS, Ph.D.
> University of Minnesota, Family Social Science
> Author of *Family Stress Management*

"I WON'T WAIT UP TONIGHT"

What to do to take care of *yourself* when you're living with an alcoholic or an addict

Terence Williams

HAZELDEN®

Hazelden Educational Materials
Center City, Minnesota 55012-0176

ISBN: 0-89486-813-6

Editor's note:
  Hazelden Educational Materials offers a variety of information on chemical dependency and related areas. Our publications do not necessarily represent Hazelden's programs, nor do they officially speak for any Twelve Step organization.
  Some of the stories of people in this book are based on the lives of actual people; some are composites based on the experiences of several people. In all cases, names have been changed and, in many cases, circumstances have been changed, to protect anonymity.

In Memoriam

Clark T.

Born to the Breed

Contents

INTRODUCTION
There Is Hope

Families are not labeled as "dysfunctional" or "codependent" in this book. Instead, these are the stories of ordinary people who are managing to cope with thoroughly human problems—alcoholism and drug addiction.

CHAPTER ONE
Home Truth: When You're Ready to Face the Facts
25

Most families, when they have to, learn how to live with problem drinking and drug abuse, as Nick and Mary's marriage illustrates. This chapter explains how the natural response of most families to alcohol and other drug abuse is to try to contain the problem.

CHAPTER TWO
How to Get Off the Merry-Go-Round
49

The bitter truth is that our anxious reactions to someone's drinking and drug abuse tend to promote more drinking and drug use. Mary discovers a new—and surprisingly effective—form of intervention.

CHAPTER THREE
Why Do Some People Become Addicted to Drugs and Alcohol?
71

In Ben and Sarah's case, you'll see that the reasons behind why people become addicted are varied and complex. Alcoholism and drug addiction simply don't lend themselves well to scientific description.

CHAPTER FOUR
Detachment: A Special Kind of Caring
95

Family members are often left with a lot of *why's* when a loved one is addicted or alcoholic, as Ben learns after Sarah enters treatment. Despite these *why's*, family members do best when they move on and learn to practice detachment.

CHAPTER FIVE
When an Older Family Member Drinks Too Much
111

Unfortunately, alcoholism and drug addiction are life and death matters—as Peter discovers in this story about his Aunt Nora, an older woman who lives alone.

CHAPTER SIX
High-Tech Drugs and Family Ties
141

Illegal drugs like cocaine can create new and alarming situations for families, as Jenny and Tom discover when their college-aged son embezzles one hundred thousand dollars from the family business. Tom and Jenny learn that they can forgive and support their son, but that only he can be responsible for his recovery. Time is a major factor in recovery for the whole family.

Acknowledgments

The wonderful families I encountered during twenty years at the Hazelden Family Center taught me most of what I know about addiction and the family. I'm grateful as well to friends and colleagues I worked with at Hazelden. Supervision by Harold Swift, ACSW, shaped my basic thinking about this subject. The late Murray Bowen, M.D., with whom I studied at the Georgetown University Family Center, showed me that coming to terms with my own family is the essential preparation for working with other families. That's a lesson I continue to learn. Rebecca Post has been an inspiring teacher as well as an editor, and I'm indebted to her. Finally, I want to thank my dear wife, Patricia Hampl.

"I Won't Wait Up Tonight"

How It Was for Me . . .

It would be great if alcohol and drug problems were neatly recognizable, quantifiable "issues." Great, too, if they didn't wreck lives, humiliate and estrange people who meant to love each other and live happily ever after. But alcoholism and drug addiction, finally, amount to story after story, fiercely held in bruised hearts. Telling the stories is the beginning of perhaps not "science," but, certainly, reality. Let me tell you how it was for me. Here's a late day in my story that bruised some hearts, including my own.

After my divorce, I moved to a place out in the Wakarusa Valley ten miles from town. It was an abandoned hardware store at a country crossroad, with an apartment in the back of the building. Farm machinery rusted in the yard among the brown winter weeds. Across the road was the hangar of a crop duster airport. Along the creek at the back there were new buds on the willow trees. Green winter wheat had begun to appear in the fields. It was a fine quiet place where I knew I could be safe. Why did I ever go out again looking for trouble? Maybe you can tell me.

During that March and April, I drove an old pickup truck to my office at the library, through the hills of the Kansas springtime countryside, always half sick with the flulike symptoms of withdrawal from nights of solitary drinking. Running on empty, I would fake it at work, overamped on coffee and amphetamines. I went through all the motions, so it all looked all right. Sort of. But I wasn't really there: I could not manage to concentrate or think or make decisions. I avoided people. Maybe I knew that the time was up; maybe I didn't.

At the end of every workday, I followed a certain ritual. I'd stop at a liquor store on the edge of town for cheap wine. There were two of these stores, and I would carefully alternate my route so neither store owner would know how much I was drinking. At the time, this seemed to be an important consideration, another piece of proof of my thoughtful social awareness. There were many of these small deceptions in my life then—my lying to myself and calling it prudence.

With the bottle in a discreet brown paper bag, I would drive to a certain point off beyond the river and park the truck. Then I would check for other cars on the road. I'd twist the cap from the bottle

and take a long beatific pull on the wine. I can remember it as if it had happened five minutes ago,
the sweet metallic taste of the wine, and then—
instantly—a cosmic and inspirational blood rush.
This was something that I could count on. It happened every time. For a few minutes, warmth
flowed through my body while I hid the bottle in
the toolbox, checked out the road again, and
headed off through the hills toward the Wakarusa
crossroad, rattling along slowly over the stretches
of washboard gravel.

I had already been arrested twice for public
drunkenness and once for driving while intoxicated. In May, I committed still another drunken
crime. There was still another blacked-out night
out in town, still another blind-drunk car-chase
fistfight with still another team of cops, still another remorse-filled, endless, miserable, and dirty
weekend in jail, and still another court appearance.
At long last, the long-suffering university asked for
my resignation. At a private reception in his sol-
emn chambers, the chancellor said he was thinking
of me and my family—this was true—as he explained something I already knew: I was no longer
an asset to the community.

I didn't even go back to empty out my desk and
files. I began staying out in the country all the
time, so drunk for so many days that I could no
longer get drunk, so tired I couldn't sleep, so sick I
couldn't eat.

I will try to explain something that happened
early on a Sunday morning a few weeks later. It

helps to know that Kansas did not sell alcohol on Sundays then. I had hidden a bottle somewhere in my own place to cover just this difficulty. But I couldn't find the bottle. Okay. That part of it is easy enough to say. But then it gets complicated, because you may not be able to understand that I had hidden the bottle from myself in the first place. Sober, even I don't understand this very well, but I know that's the way it was. I bought the bottle so I wouldn't be caught short on Sunday, and I hid it from myself. Two facts. Two seemingly opposing facts.

The act of hiding the bottle was at least partly to guarantee that I'd have something to drink in the morning, so I'd know there was a bottle there, somewhere. It gave me a sense of security, of being in control of my life. It was just another ritual routine. It was a part of my own particular drinking M.O. I don't like to think what Freud might have called it. And then, of course, I had hidden the bottle because I didn't want anyone else to know I was still drinking—my children, the landlord, my ex-wife, or any of the few friends (on the way to being former friends) who might come by.

It's also hard to explain how I felt when I couldn't find that lost bottle. For an hour and a half I searched behind all the books and papers in the bookcase, through the confusion of the clothes closet, in the battered chest of drawers, through the shelves of the kitchen cupboards, in the bed, under the bed, and in the sheets. I had looked in the bottom of the sleeping bag, under the toilet, in

the toilet tank, and behind the shower curtain. I
had checked out every last one of the dusty shelves
and all the bins and boxes in every cupboard and
cabinet in the abandoned hardware store in the
front part of the building. And I had looked under
the seats and all through the cab of the truck and
inside and under the engine compartment, and
through every pile of weeds and wood and every
piece of junk in the yard—every last place I could
possibly have put it. I was absolutely frantic. I was
close to being suicidal. I was out there in the side
yard, wildly throwing gear out of the truck while I
searched through it for the third or fourth time,
when the county judge drove up.

Before I could think about what he was doing
there, my immediate reaction was to pull myself together, quick as an animal, and pretend that I was
cleaning up the truck, a perfectly normal thing to
be doing on a Sunday morning in the country,
right? He sat in his car for a moment, looked up,
and acknowledged me without smiling. Slowly and
deliberately, he closed his car door and headed my
way. We shook hands, and he said he could just
stay a few minutes.

Judge Folwell was a fair man, everyone said. I
knew him. My ex-wife and I had seen him two or
three times at parties. I had voted for him. I had
appeared in court before him three times in the
past six months, and I was due to see him there
again soon. More than fair, he was scrupulously
fair. His vision of life was refracted through a lens
of the law so clearly and logically that he could

have judged his own uncle—though maybe not his own son—fairly. And there I was, "the alcoholic," on a warm Sunday summertime morning, in a state of absolute stone panic, trying to appear normal before this fair man.

When I looked at John Folwell that morning, I did not see a man. It was Society itself that had come out to the country to see me. And Society, while it might be willing to shake my hand, was unable to give me a smile. As the university chancellor had said when he fired me from my tenured position, I was no longer, by any stretch of the imagination, an asset to the community. In what I sensed might be its last visit to me, Society only had a few minutes to spare.

Judge Folwell says he wants me to know that people are worried about me. He doesn't say family or friends: "People," he says. And he doesn't explain. And I don't ask. So, I understand that this isn't the judge's usual way of doing business. Somehow I'm feeling grateful that he has come so far out of his way to see me. He goes on to say, "Now, there are two or three things we can do. You know, of course—and I don't want to worry you about this today—that some time in the lockup is a real possibility. I don't suppose that would be of much help right now, given the shape you're in, and I don't imagine it would help matters much in the long run. But that has to be considered as a possibility. I just want you to realize—I know that you do realize—that we've got a genuine problem here." My heart was sinking. That's the accurate way to describe it. Literally, I could feel my heart beating hard and sinking toward my stomach.

"Now, people are asking me to consider another possibility. And this is another thing that I wanted to tell you about. Some people are thinking pretty seriously that we should send you off to the State Hospital. They're worried about what you might do to yourself." I stood before him, sweating, tremulous, dry-mouthed, heart pounding, desperate for a drink, and I assured him that, yes, everything was fine and, no, I wouldn't do anything dangerous.

"Now," he continued, "the State Hospital isn't what it once was. You know that, I guess. You also know those folks over in Topeka. They've made some changes there. And that might be another solution to consider. I don't want you to tell me what you might think about that just yet. If you're all right now, then there's some time, and it can wait.

"But," he went on, "the third thing is that I want to ask you if you can handle this problem any other way. I know that you were in a treatment clinic a year ago, and it seemed to help for a while. Now, tell me, do you suppose there's anything like that that you can do now to take care of this problem? Now, I can't stick around. But I just want you to give all of this some thought before we have to take some action."

For all these many years, I've said to myself that my family was unable to get me to shape up, that even losing my job didn't do it, that it finally took the long arm of the law to help me see the light.

But, of course, that isn't true. In fact, my ex-wife had finally found the courage to step away from my problem and give it back to me. So had other family members and friends. And the long-suffering university, which had given me every chance, finally did the same thing. When Judge Folwell drove up on that Sunday morning, he was just carrying the message that I had already been given by everyone else who cared about me.

This time, I listened. I can't claim to know why. There are no easy explanations for our problems. And sometimes, it's just as difficult to explain the solutions. But it happened. Somehow, I was able to hear. Call it grace, call it luck, call it exhaustion, but somehow it happened. I suppose that hidden bottle is out there still, lying in the weeds, the label rotted off, the alcohol still good.

INTRODUCTION

There Is Hope

This is a guidebook for those of you who are preoccupied with the behavior of people you are devoted to, the people you think of as your family. It's for those of you whose devotion causes you to overreact when alcohol and other drug-related problems seem to threaten to overwhelm you. And it's for those of you who quietly and grimly adjust your lives and adapt to these problems day by day, trying to make everything work out. It's also for everyone in between, all of you who are concerned about the alcohol and other drug abuse, real or imagined, of people in your families.

First, let's think for a minute about what the family is in the 1990s. We live in exciting times for the institution of the family. Some would say that these are perilous times. Young people especially, but many oldsters, too, are redefining the concept of "the family" so radically that some social scientists predict that soon we will have no families at all. True, perhaps, if we limit our thinking about families to the concept of the traditional American family. From that point of view, the statistics do seem to be ominous. Not long ago, we would have said that "the family" was the housewife mom, the breadwinner pop, plus a couple of kids. Today, this description fits only one family in ten.

A substantial part of the population today will experience marriage, divorce, and remarriage, while millions of children live in single-parent families. Millions of people are living alone now, and still other millions live together in various kinds of devoted relationships, without marrying.

I believe that those who are making ominous predictions about the death of the family as an institution are just whistling "Dixie." They may be unable to appreciate all the adjustments that new families are making in order to survive in this age. Instead of predicting the death of the family, I think we could more usefully look at this era as a period of experimentation and reorientation in family life. On really good days, it even looks like a renaissance of family life, newly defined and ordered by dynamic relationships.

We look around us and see various and interesting substitute families. We are all trying to work out the best solutions that we can. Our basic spiritual beliefs about family relationships are still at the very heart of the matter. Our biology still informs our beliefs. We continue to adapt to cultural changes that are taking place with breathtaking speed. We're still getting together, in imaginative new ways, trying to stay in the game in the Disneyland we all live in.

THE TIES THAT BIND

The word *family* has a special emotional meaning to us. It carries a charge that no other word carries. And I will use *family* in this book in a very broad way to refer to people with whom we have important and continuing relationships—the traditional family plus some kith and kin. In other words, the people whom we have thrown in with. In these new relationship systems, our emotional ties as well as our practical ties may be more brittle than they are in traditional families, but they can be very strong. If someone we are devoted to seems to be having trouble with alcohol and other drugs, we feel and act like "family"—whatever the nature of the ties that bind us.

Over the years, I've learned from the families who have come to the Hazelden Family Center how difficult it is to face up to problem drinking and drug abuse, to alcoholism and other drug addiction. I know about the fears and doubts you feel, your anger and frustration, your weariness, and your sheer despair. I've also seen your love and dedication. I've seen your patience, tolerance, and understanding. And I have seen your optimism in the face of problems that you can't seem to pin down and that you seem unable to do anything about.

And I've seen, although I really can't explain it, the wonderful and mysterious process that people go through when they regain self-confidence, find new directions for themselves, and eventually discover, looking back on it all, that managing to cope with this problem has enriched their lives. I want to pass on some of the things that I've learned from troubled families over the years, some things that you may find to be helpful.

STATISTICS OF DESPAIR

Experts say that alcohol dependence by itself is the most common medical and psychiatric problem in the United States today. Harmful dependence on both legal and illegal drugs other than alcohol must surely be high on the list as well. There may never be an objective way to assess the terrible pain and misery that families experience because of alcohol and other drug problems. Will we ever be able to comprehend such anguish?

We do, however, have some figures that attempt to tally up the economic costs to the nation of alcoholism and other drug dependence. A Department of Health and Human Services report, *The Economic Costs of Alcohol, Drug Abuse and Mental Illness*, published in 1990, indicates that alcohol dependence cost the nation $70.3 billion in the year

1985. In the same year, the costs for coping with dependence on drugs other than alcohol added up to $44.1 billion. These figures include the costs of lost worker productivity, expenditures for law enforcement, and the costs of education, prevention, and for the treatment and support of people with alcoholism and drug addiction.

Alcohol and drug problems are about all these alarming facts and figures, the statistics of despair that assault us in the news media. But there's much more to it than these statistics. Almost everyone in this country is personally involved, at one time or another, with the problem of addiction. And in this special way, addiction isn't a remote and abstract problem described in statistical summaries. It isn't even the sum of the terrible things we see on television or read about in the newspapers. I want to address the problems of addiction that affect us personally—addictions that involve our children, our friends and neighbors, the people that we work with, our husbands and wives—our own families.

HOW MUCH IS TOO MUCH?

Addictions are so essentially a part of the human dilemma that they are difficult for us to define in any truly scientific way. Who among us isn't somewhat addicted to something or other, or too much dependent sometimes? And how much is too much?

Is it just social drinking? Experimentation with drugs? Or is it rebellious acting out? Serious preoccupation? Harmful obsession? Physical or psychological addiction? Who knows? And where do you draw the lines? And who draws them? And for whom? Just exactly how dependent do you have to be to be too dependent? We will get back to this subject in the pages that follow.

WHY I'M WRITING THIS BOOK

I'm writing this book for those of you who are coping with the undeniable fact of problem drinking and drug abuse, but I'm also writing it for those who only imagine that alcohol and other drugs are a central problem. In terms of how families live, it doesn't seem to matter much whether Dad is an alcoholic—or if everybody is just jumpy about his drinking. Either way, the problem is there. The family dynamics are pretty much the same in either case.

I will give you some information about addiction as I understand it. However, I won't encourage you to become diagnosticians. If the abuse of alcohol and other drugs by someone in your family is serious enough to get you upset about it, you will find some useful information here. I won't set you up to label people—yourself, your family, or anyone else.

There won't be any discussion in this book of "codependency," for example. No attempt will be made to describe symptoms of either the little children or the adult children of alcoholics. Troubled families will not be referred to in these pages as being dysfunctional. Instead of explaining to you how sick you may be, I will try to point out how you can resolve some of the problems you face.

In my clinical experience, it isn't the categories of symptomatic problems that have been so interesting. Instead, it's been inspiring to see the imagination and resilience and resourcefulness people demonstrate when they face difficulties. The troubled families I have worked with have constantly renewed my own faith in human nature.

Intellectually tempting as they are, diagnostic categories unfortunately tend to suggest that whole groups of people are the same, somehow. The families I've worked with have had similar experiences, with similar situations, it's true. These similar experiences help them to understand one another. But the truly important things they share with others are their faith, hope, and charity. In fact, the variations and nuances of each family experience *are* the family. Categories and labels tend to obscure this essential fact.

In order to illustrate some of these basic situations that are common to many families, I've drawn on the stories of a few typical people from the thousands who have come to the Hazelden Family Center. I've put people, geography, and even whole anecdotes and episodes into a narrative blender in order to preserve anonymity. Still, while these tales are stories, they are also true. I've known these families, these scenes.

There are five specific things I would like to accomplish in these pages:

1. To give you definitions of problem drinking and drug abuse, and of alcoholism and drug addiction, together with some ideas about the process of recovery.

2. To help you assess realistically how you may be caught up in someone else's addictive patterns.

3. To give you some ideas that will help you plan how to break out of these patterns and cope with your problems more effectively.

4. To encourage you to make balanced, thoughtful, and effective decisions about your life rather than repetitive patterned reactions to each new crisis.

5. To help you see your way through difficult times without too much damage being done to you or to the person you care about.

CLOSE TO HOME

Alcoholism and addiction are hot topics that are very troubling to everyone involved: to become upset about this kind of problem is normal. I hope you will realize that millions of others know this problem, too, and that you will find some small comfort in the fact that you are not alone. My intention is to offer information that will clear up some of the mysteries. I urge you to seek the support of other people who understand what you are going through, and I'll try to point you in the direction of this kind of help.

Alcohol and other drug problems threaten the very fabric of the nation. We are all aware of that truth as an abstract concept, as a piece of information. The media regularly provide us with vivid illustrations of the terrible human suffering that alcoholism and addiction produce. The press, books, films, the theater, and television show us junkies probing collapsed veins; old men sleeping on sidewalks, wrapped in newspapers, clutching wine bottles; paramedics pounding life back into "code blue" victims of overdose; inner-city kids with dead eyes sniffing glue in alleys; stockbrokers snorting coke in airport toilets; drunk drivers staggering away from fatal accidents. The media bring all these images into our living rooms, so we don't get hurt and we don't get dirty. Instead, the events portrayed remain abstractions that we comment on to one another, often after a professional commentary by a news analyst.

In our daily lives, most of us are several steps closer than this to concerns about alcohol and other drugs. It isn't as cool as it once was to get stoned. We at least think about appointing a designated driver

when we go out for the evening. We're alarmed that
children are drinking wine coolers as if they were sodas. We wonder if it's safe to take the subway at certain times of night. We worry about airline pilots
who might have been drinking before flying the
plane we're on.

We get involved in school and neighborhood
social-action projects to make life more difficult for
drug dealers. We ask ourselves if liquor bottles
should have warning labels on them. We know it's
okay to order soft drinks at a bar instead of alcohol.
Women are avoiding alcohol and other drugs during their pregnancies. There are wines instead of
hard liquor at dinner parties. The heat is on athletes who use drugs, and on businesspeople who
drink at lunch. The good old boys are drinking light
beer now. There's a genuine awareness across the
land that we need to be serious about alcohol and
other drugs.

Closer still to our hearts and homes, most of us
have heard stories about people we know who have
alcohol and other drug problems, people who we
might or might not describe as addicts. People at
the office will talk about a business acquaintance
who has six tranquilizer prescriptions from six different physicians. Or you may have a friend everyone thinks is a little drunk when he drives over to
pick up the children after school. Half of the class
knows about the medical student who uses all his
own pharmaceutical samples and borrows others
from colleagues. Your neighbor, a cross-country
trucker, may boast about knowing coast-to-coast in-

terstate amphetamine networks. You may think that people among a certain group of high school athletes are dealing drugs. Your uncle heard that the farm down the road is for sale because one child snorted the family's entire bank line of credit up his nose last year.

Once upon a time, a lot of us might have said, "That kind of thing could never happen to us." Now, with alcohol and other drug problems so much in the media, I think we're all aware that these problems could very well turn up in our families—and they do. It's reasonable to suppose that you, too, have a story about how alcohol and other drugs have affected your relationships with others in your own family, or with people that you're close to.

The basic purpose of this book is to help you understand that you are not alone if you are concerned about someone's abuse of alcohol and other drugs. Others have had experiences enough like yours to understand how you feel. By telling you about them, maybe I can give you some ideas that will help you to do a better job of coping with your problems. Or maybe, in reading these case histories, you'll discover you're doing pretty well already.

I hope that reading this book will encourage you to trust your own judgment a bit more. That's my biggest hope—and my best faith. Without this faith in your good common sense and the gift of my years of working with families, I couldn't write this guidebook. In the chapters that follow you'll find some new ideas about how to improve the quality of your life through hearing about the successes and the failures of others who have been there.

CHAPTER ONE

Home Truth:
When You're Ready
to Face the Facts

NICK

The smell of Lysol turns his stomach. Nick shivers under an old army blanket on a narrow iron cot. Half-conscious, he turns his head to see the barred door, toilet, and sink in the corner. Through the small window of the cell, a gray winter sky, rooftops of factories—but what city? Rumble of traffic on streets below. He pulls himself up, lights a half-crushed cigarette. Is anyone else here? Totally alert now, he realizes he is still drunk. He feels sick and gags, wants to vomit but can't. His topcoat sleeve is torn, his watch is gone. Steam clanks through cold radiators. My God, where am I? What have I done? What day is this? What time is it?

A long time passes. He's too terrified to shout for help. Then, a steel door clangs open at the end of the empty corridor. The turnkey's boot steps ring out as he walks toward Nick's cell and unlocks the gate. Military eyes look right through Nick with no expression and turn away. Now, the two men move out and down the row of cells, out of the cell block, directly into a warm courtroom to stand before the judge. A cop testifies that he found Nick passed out in his parked car on Signal Hill. So, he's in Detroit, forty miles from home. "Public drunkenness. Bail is set at $250. Next case."

The wall clock reads 9:15. Having some facts now helps Nick begin to put things together. Yesterday afternoon he was in the city to discuss a building project with a client. He planned to be back home by 7:30 last night. He was supposed to meet his staff this morning at 9:00 to begin writing a new project proposal. Tonight there's a special meeting of the church vestry. What am I going to tell Mary?

MARY

It's 4:00 A.M., and Mary sits at the kitchen table. Her hands clasp a mug of coffee. She and Nick had planned to have a quiet dinner together late, after the children were in bed. She waited for him for an hour, then ate her meal without him. She wearily washed the dishes and put everything away. She called a good friend who might have known where

Nick was, without asking her anything directly, but she didn't find out where he could be.

She watched a "Nightline" debate on arms control. She watched "The Tonight Show." There were cold and homeless people on the late news, and she cried. She found she couldn't concentrate on the midnight movie, and she turned off the TV. She tried to do the *New York Times* crossword. She tried to read. She tried to rest on the couch, even slept fitfully. In three hours the kids have to get up. Three hours! If I don't have my report finished tomorrow, I can forget about a raise. What can I do with three hours? Oh, Nick, you bastard! I hope you're not hurt. I wish you were dead. What's happening to us? Either you're gone or you're drunk. It's not a life any longer for any of us—not for you, not for me, not for the kids, not even for the damned dog!

WHAT TO TELL MARY?

Bail is set at $250. The judge cracked his gavel. Next case. When he heard these solemn words, Nick's panic level cranked down one notch. Through the cold early morning in his jail cell, he anguished about the blacked-out night before. Now, he tries to stand straight and hold himself together long enough to figure out what to do next. He'll call his attorney, Bill, as soon as he can. It's not a nightmare, but it's bad. After he gets Bill, he'll call the office. Or should he call the office first? Can he explain that he mixed up his dates and has just now realized his mistake? No, first he needs help here. It looks as if there wasn't an accident. His car must have been impounded. Where the hell is his watch? Mary! Is it better to tell her he spent the night in jail or to make up some other excuse? What excuse? What can he tell Mary? He's got to call her. His head is clearing now. He's starting to take charge again.

HOW WILL I COVER FOR HIM THIS TIME?

Mary phones her own office and tells them she's sick. Then she calls Nick's secretary with a too-elaborate story of family illness and out-of-town travel. She knows they both know why Nick isn't at the office. It's a charade they both take part in, both of these women who take care of Nick. He needs the explanations, and Mary provides them, always, and the secretary honors them, always.

Nick isn't as good a diplomat as Mary is. Diplomat, she says to herself; maybe liar is more like it. She tells the children that Nick has had to work late in the city and has stayed overnight there. Then she straightens up the house, washes the breakfast dishes, makes all the beds, and takes a bath. She lies down on the couch, finally, and sleeps.

Some time later, she wakes all of a sudden, in a panic. She's filled with fear and rage: another damned mess to clear up. What are we going to do?

This has to stop, she says to herself. She'll take the kids and leave Nick. This time, by God, she'll do it. And then, just as suddenly, all of her angry energy seems to drain away. Now she feels very sorry for Nick, sorry for all of them—very sorry about it all. And then her mood shifts again, and she is terribly afraid. How will they take care of the children? What will happen to them all? How will I cover for him this time? she thinks. She is totally exhausted now, but her thoughts keep her awake.

WHERE DID WE GO WRONG?

Nick and Mary both came from families that drank socially. Both of them experienced the conventional Middle West, middle-class rites of passage involving alcohol, rituals that both condemned and paradoxically celebrated alcohol. In tune with their times, both of them had experimented with other drugs as well when they were younger.

Drinking was a part of their end-of-the-day times together and of their parties and picnics with family, friends, and neighbors. Sure, once in a while Nick got really loaded, but not that often, and, after all, wasn't getting loaded fairly normal, just once in a while? Who sets the standards for these things anyway?

Good question. Normal social drinking can turn into serious problem drinking over a course of time with no one knowing what has happened. During

their courtship, Mary and Nick established some
basic unwritten rules regarding drinking, one of
which was that Nick could drink irresponsibly if he
didn't carry it too far. Neither one said anything
about this, but the agreement was quietly made between them at an early date. Another unwritten
rule was that Mary would always stay sober
enough to see they didn't have too much trouble.

Subconsciously, Nick knew just about how much
of his drinking Mary could tolerate, and, relent-
lessly, he stretched this limit. He was entirely
guileless in all of this. In fact, that's the way it
worked. Mary fought to maintain what she thought
were reasonable standards about drinking, but she
was forever retreating, giving ground graciously,
fitfully, little by little. During all their years together, they led an active social life, and Mary
would have had a hard time figuring out just when
it all began to get out of hand.

Even now, lying sleepless on the couch, Mary has
begun planning the damage control strategy, trying
to figure out how to put this latest one behind
them.

She protected Nick from the children when they
were wild, and she protected the children from
Nick when his moods were unpredictable. His
drinking was a factor she had to consider as she or-
ganized their social calendar. And she kept him
very much in mind when she made holiday plans to
be with their families. More and more often she
found that she was appointing herself as "designated driver" when they were out for the evening.

When the children were upset, Mary worried that she wasn't a good mother. She wondered to herself if Nick drank because she had failed him somehow. Oftentimes, especially when she was alone in the night, waiting for him to come home, she thought about all of this. Was she really right for him? Would he be a different person if she hadn't married him?

Her feelings of inadequacy were especially strong during visits with Nick's parents—the perfect couple, as she and Nick called them. They came to see their grandchildren several times a year, and Mary sometimes felt they were there all year round. They were both from families that felt a wife's primary job was to support her husband. Mary's career was acceptable, but just barely. On two or three occasions, Mary had to ask Nick's parents for help to get him out of trouble. His mother subtly implied that he might not have been in trouble if Mary weren't preoccupied with her own career.

IS THIS REALLY THE LAST STRAW?

Her own parents, two thousand miles away in Texas, were usually open and frank about family matters—and outspoken. During occasional visits, and during frequent long phone conversations, they always made it clear to Mary that they supported her. In the past year or two, as Nick's drinking became more problematic, her parents reacted strongly to Mary's accounts of his troubles.

Late in the fall, Mary and Nick drove with the children to Texas for a vacation. Mary's parents made a point of not having beer in the refrigerator. And they gave Nick a long temperance lecture. Now Mary feels she has to be careful about what she tells her parents, and that doesn't feel right to her. She's trying with all her diplomacy to save the marriage. Her parents keep telling her, and they tell Nick, too, that enough is enough. Is something deep within her encouraging her to say to these up-front parents who are very supportive of her, "Look! Enough already. I'm a grown-up now and I can handle this one!"

But is she really able to handle this one? Mary tosses and turns. She's furious, and she's afraid. Is this really the last straw? Is this even more than she can handle, on top of everything else that's happened during the past few months? It's really all too much—their dangerous loud fights that make the children cry, the embarrassing arguments with neighbors, the sick hangovers, all the work that Nick has missed, and all of the excuses she has made for him. She's afraid of his angry moods. She's even afraid now of her own growing resentments.

Nick has had two DWIs, and she worries constantly about his driving; there's an unspoken rule that he won't pick up the children after school now. Both she and Nick pretend the children don't know how bad things really are. She worries that their friends and neighbors will find out just how badly their life is going.

Like Nick, she is preoccupied now with the idea that his company will find out how much he drinks, how often he is drunk, what a serious problem he really has. Everyone at the office knows that Nick drinks too much sometimes. He drinks even when no one else does. Drinking just isn't as acceptable as it once was at the company. No one has the fabled two- or three-martini lunch anymore. In fact, no one drinks martinis, even Nick. But he has wine when everyone else is drinking coffee and sodas, and she has heard people comment about this.

If Nick ever lost his job . . . Oh, my God, if that ever happened, what would we do? Nick really does have a drinking problem, doesn't he? Mary's mind races. Am I overreacting? But we can't go on this way. I can't let the children go through any more of this. Maybe it isn't as bad as I think. Do I have an overly active imagination? Am I making too much of Nick's drinking? No, no, no. Damn, damn, damn it all!

LIVING *AROUND* THE PROBLEM

Let's face it, most families, when they have to, can learn how to live with problem drinking and drug abuse. Over the time that it often takes for full-blown alcoholism and drug addiction to develop, if it comes to that, they can adjust some

more, and learn to live with the next stage of difficulty. The natural response of most families to alcohol and drug problems is to contain the problems
and try to solve them at home.

Years ago, I interviewed a young woman with a
small baby who had come to a street agency where
I worked. She was looking for help for her heroin-
addicted husband. Back in those days, when I
didn't understand much and would still ask dumb
questions like this, I asked her how she managed
to put up with her husband's neglect and abuse.

She said, "You just learn to live *around* it all."
And she went on to explain that she would avoid
him when he was upset, that she didn't depend on
him much for food and shelter, and that she and
her daughter tried to enjoy whatever part of his
companionship he was able to give them. She didn't
reach out for help until things got so rough that
she just couldn't handle the situation any longer.
Her husband had finally begun to beat her regularly, and she was afraid that he would hurt their
daughter, too.

Peter Steinglass, M.D., is a psychiatrist who has
conducted important research on the subject of alcoholism and the family. What he has to say about
alcoholism fits with what we also know about other
drug abuse and addictions. He and his colleagues
say that we tend to focus our attention on the dramatic alcohol-related family problems such as
abuse and violence, divorce and desertions, serious
domestic crimes and other disasters. These are the
stories that make the news. And he contends that

we don't pay enough attention to the plight of all the many families that are living *around* the problem—all those troubled families whose situations never make the headlines, the ones who are dying by inches as alcohol and drug problems slowly erode the quality of their family life.

How many millions of people suffer with addictions for years because the addict's behavior is tempered to stay just barely within the limits that the family can adjust to? Addicts manage somehow to stop short of causing enough trouble to prompt the family to take action. For their part, family members will adjust their family routines and their social habits to accommodate the addict. Everyone living with alcoholism and drug abuse learns to be careful. This carefulness, ironically, is the source of the devastating long-term and chronic nature of the problem. Typically, everyone is so careful that no one ever does anything to go after the problem head-on. No one blows the whistle, so the problem is never addressed for what it is.

Sometimes alcoholism and drug addiction can very subtly and persistently become the most important problems that families have to cope with, and all the while these people don't even know what's actually happening. Maybe illnesses and injuries seem to plague a family. Maybe financial difficulties are dragging them down. Maybe they're suffering from the strains of stress reaction and emotional problems. Often, problems like these may actually be the end results of long-term alcohol and other drug abuse, and the families themselves have failed to make the connection.

DENIAL OR PRUDENCE?

Typically, in troubled families like Mary and Nick's, alcohol is a normal part of family life for years before it becomes a problem. Still more years may pass before the problem is recognized for what it is. We're tempted to say that people who live with alcohol problems are denying reality, that they're "into denial," but it isn't as simple as that.

It may be more accurate to say that the alcohol problems become a central part of the reality that some families experience, and that as a result, alcoholism becomes, for such people, strangely invisible. To look at it another way, when they begin to experience a chronic situation like alcoholism or addiction, families focus all their efforts on containing the problem and are unable to see that these efforts simply prolong the problem.

Even when someone's drinking behavior is truly off the wall, it's very tough for a couple to admit this to one another, not to mention acknowledging it to the children. It's often difficult for people to agree on what to do about it. If the immediate family can get together and decide that something must be done, the alcoholic may have other ideas about the situation. "I'll quit tomorrow," he may say, in one complex, complicated, and convoluted way or another.

WHY IT'S HARD TO GET HELP

If, finally, everyone does agree to look for help, there's the very integrity of the family to be considered, your security and income, plans for the future for yourself and your children, all of which may be threatened if you acknowledge this problem and reach out for help.

The standards and values that two people bring together from their own separate family histories figure into what's going to be done or left undone about alcoholism in their own marriage and home life. From one generation to the next, the parents, the grandparents, and all the various aunts, uncles, and cousins have a powerful say in these matters, magically. We understand through their teaching and their examples, through the stories that they've passed on about how they have lived their lives, how things have worked out in their families, even how they've dealt with the issue of addiction.

For instance, if it's a tradition that has existed over generations in a family for the women to put up with the problem drinking of their husbands, it's very difficult to break away from that pattern, even as the new public health information encourages temperance, and even as feminism encourages women to become more assertive.

Other complicating factors are our relationships with all of our friends and neighbors—our social networks, people in our communities who help us define what everyday work and life are all about. Can we risk upsetting the apple cart by getting honest and coming to terms with our problems? What will they think of us? Do they really know how bad this problem is? If they knew, would they understand and support us? Will we lose friendships? Will we be unable to find insurance? Could we have trouble obtaining a mortgage? Maybe even lose a job?

Thoughts like these race through Mary's mind as she lies exhausted and sleepless on the couch. Even though she is still filled with doubts, she realizes that she has reached the end of the tether. She thinks about the children, and she looks to the future. And she begins to know that she must do something to stop this madness.

HOW MUCH IS TOO MUCH?

The big question that still troubles Mary in spite of all the evidence is: Is he really an alcoholic? Is it really an addiction, or am I just imagining all this and blowing it all out of proportion? It's true that most alcoholics have trouble admitting their alcoholism. It's also true that family members have al-

most the same amount of trouble, even as they rage
against the daily fears and humiliations implicit in
the situation.

Family members, even if they have good information, may be unable to recognize the symptoms of
addiction to alcohol and other drugs for what they
are. A good practical guideline, according to Dr.
Daniel Anderson of the Hazelden Foundation, is:
"An alcoholic or an addict is someone who uses alcohol or other drugs inappropriately, who suffers
harmful consequences as a result, and who then repeats the inappropriate use of the substance."

But just what is inappropriate? How does a family figure this out? How much is actually too much?
What if your family and the other people you grew
up with haven't given you a good idea about what
is okay and what isn't okay when it comes to alcohol use? And whose rules do you follow if you've
moved to a new part of the country? Or if you've re-
located into a new neighborhood? And how about
the fact that times have changed? And what if you
hang around with a different crowd from the kind
of people you grew up with? Who's making all the
rules anyway?

Not only do different families have different
standards, there are also community standards
about appropriate and inappropriate alcohol use
that can vary greatly from one place to another.
This country is truly a melting pot on this issue,
and different cultures have different views of what
kind of drinking is okay.

A family in Nevada, the state with the highest

rate of alcohol consumption in the nation, might have one idea about what is inappropriate use of alcohol. Meanwhile, a neighbor across the line in Utah, which has the lowest rate, may have an entirely different idea about the matter. If you want one etiquette book that lays downs the rules for social drinking in America, you will have a hard time finding it.

What it all boils down to, finally, is that most of us make up our own minds about how to use alcohol and other drugs appropriately, even if our own rules don't agree with everyone else's. After a point, we don't really need someone else to explain the rules. Still, the process of deciding that a person we care about is an alcoholic, deciding that he or she drinks so much that we need to blow the whistle, is a terrible problem for families.

It is difficult to make a rational assessment when there are few clear standards. This is a large part of the problem. The rest of the problem is that we don't want to take it upon ourselves to say that someone's behavior is inappropriate, even if we're pretty sure that it is, even if we see someone destroying himself or herself, even if the behavior is threatening us. This is another of the reasons why families suffer with problem drinking for so long.

Families put up with alcohol and other drug problems because, first, they don't want to believe that these problems exist, and second, because it's difficult during the early stages of addiction to convince themselves and others that someone is an addict. Finally, if they do know that someone is an addict, it's difficult to figure out what to do about it. There usually seems to be more judgment around than help.

A FAMILY AFFAIR

A new approach to coping with alcoholism and other drug addictions means getting the whole family involved in the process of recovery. As some background information, I want to mention just a few of the prominent modern pioneers who knew how important the family is to our understanding of alcoholism and addiction. These people recognized the needs of families who are trying to cope with addiction. They also devised new ways to help them.

These pioneers include, first and foremost, Lois W. and the people who helped her to organize the Al-Anon Family Groups. There are others as well: a social worker at the University of Washington named Joan Jackson who wrote *The Adjustment of the Family to the Crisis of Alcoholism*; an Episcopal priest from North Carolina, Joseph Kellerman, whose most famous publication is *Alcoholism: A Merry-Go-Round Named Denial*; and a psychiatrist at Georgetown University, the late Murray Bowen, M.D. Dr. Bowen, with Nathan Ackerman, was one of the fathers of modern family systems theory. He has done significant work with mental illness and has also written about addictions.

These people, and other therapists who have followed, have recognized that everyone in the family has an important influence on how every other family member functions, and that everyone in the family can play an important part in the process of recovery.

Not too long ago, the troubled family was considered to be the responsibility of the social worker, whose task it was to assist and advise them and to keep them from interfering with the relationship between the doctor and the identified problem person. Today, instead of isolating patients in treatment, whole families are urged to participate in therapy sessions that help them all to resolve emotional conflicts, to improve communication, to solve various living problems, and to enrich the quality of their family life.

This new approach is part of a pattern of social change that has begun to affect many aspects of life. Fathers are encouraged to take part in the birth of children. Educational programs now teach families how to cope with chronic illnesses such as cancer, heart disease, diabetes, schizophrenia, and Alzheimer's disease. There are support groups for people whose loved ones have experienced radical surgeries, other groups for families with congenital health problems, and still other groups in which families help one another cope with alcoholism and addiction. America has begun to "think family" about many issues.

The pioneers mentioned have helped to bring about this new approach of involving the whole family in the treatment of alcoholism and drug addiction. And this may be one of the most significant developments in this special area of health care in the past fifty years. These pioneers recognized that the alcoholic and the addict always operate within the context of a social group; most typically in our culture, this is the family. Bowen explains further that alcoholism is apt to occur most often in families that are most susceptible to anxiety.

The exciting thing about getting the whole family into the act is that we don't have to wait for the addicted person to change. We know that changes we make in ourselves can powerfully influence changes in the family.

INSISTENCE-RESISTANCE

Heavy drinking by one or two family members can focus the anxiety of the rest of the family, which reacts emotionally. When trouble first starts to be apparent, the family may become guarded and careful, overly observant and overly sensitive to one another. Some family members may then become critical, intrusive, and overly involved. Finally, certain family members may begin to become manipulative and controlling as they attempt to get things straightened out.

The drinker then reacts to the family's anxiety with more drinking, maybe at an increased level of intensity, and the family will then respond with more anxiety, more criticisms and complaints, and more controlling behavior. In their very efforts to make things better, anxious families like these often make the situation even worse, in spite of themselves. Drinking and anxious family reactions, causing more reactive drinking, can spiral into serious chronic patterns. Such troubled families just can't seem to break out of these patterns once they become firmly established.

The process of family anxiety and reaction is all pretty normal behavior for most families. It's the age-old pattern of insistence and resistance. Imagine being caught up in a somewhat parallel example: you're driving the car, and you're not aware that you're going a little too fast. Then your spouse or one of your children asks you to slow down. How would you react? Some people are glad to be reminded to drive carefully, but many of us, I think, would react with some defiance, maybe with a comment about backseat drivers.

What kind of reaction do you elicit when you insist that your children eat their vegetables? What happens when you get anxious and try to insist that family members come home on time, or not talk on the phone too long, or whatever? The more anxious you get and the harder you try, the more resistance you get, right?

The only difference between the anxiety that builds up in daily household family interactions and the insistence-resistance anxiety that we're talking about here is this: alcohol and other mood-altering drugs convert the game into something much more serious than who eats vegetables, something that is a whole lot tougher—with what may become life-or-death stakes.

Sometimes strong family members or friends or the family doctor or the boss—employers and physicians have a lot of clout—can manage to overpower the alcoholic or the addict and force change. They do this through their sheer persistence, strength, or determination, or they do it by emotionally ganging up on the problem person, using threats and coercion.

And then, crisis situations can build up until they become so critical that families have to take a heavy-handed approach. Sometimes planned confrontations, commitments to hospitals or treatment centers, and threats and coercion are necessary to save lives. But this kind of thing can be a very hard way to go. And it can take a lot out of all the people who are involved. And, often, it simply doesn't work. In any event, it does not always make for happy family times.

All too often the hard confrontation becomes just an exaggerated version of a familiar and depressing family dynamic that has become a set pattern over time—the spouse, friend, or relative insists that the problem person quit drinking or using other drugs, and the problem person defiantly resists the insistence. If your own situation allows you the time to think carefully about how all these powerful interpersonal dynamics work in families—in any family— maybe you can begin to see that there are other strategies that you can employ to improve your situation. In the next chapter, you'll discover different types of strategies that can help you cope with a family member's drug or alcohol problem.

CHAPTER TWO

*How to Get Off
the Merry-Go-Round*

To return to Mary and Nick's story, we realize that they have just now experienced another crisis. Both of them are doing everything they can to smooth things out and get past the crisis, just as they have done so many times before. There is a difference this time, however. Though she still feels some ambivalence, Mary now seems pretty determined to do something about Nick's drinking problem in order to prevent him from hurting the family any further. Mary is ready to intervene.

Given a situation like this, it would be natural for Mary to ask first, "What are we going to do about Nick? Can we plan an intervention to get him into treatment?" That's a normal thing to ask, and it's very hard to put that question aside. However, remember that in Nick and Mary's case, we're dealing with the dragged-out chronic problem of alcoholism. It has dogged this family for ten years. Simply because Mary has acknowledged the situation doesn't mean she's entered into a state of emergency. There's probably still some time to work with.

We can honestly say that one form of intervention has already taken place, because Mary has decided to change the game. She doesn't yet know what she's going to do, but she's not going to continue to ride the same horse on this merry-go-round. The first essential intervention has been in her own attitude.

WHERE'S NICK?

After Nick had picked up his car at the impound lot in Detroit, he stopped at a liquor store for a bottle of white wine. He drank it as he drove the freeway home. That was about the only thing he could drink with the hangover he had. He finally reached home late in the morning to find Mary waiting for him in the living room looking frightened, exhausted, angry, and, in her usual way, somewhat resigned. All of this was familiar to him by now. He dreaded seeing her this way. He especially dreaded that look of resignation. He read it as judgment of him, or the step beyond judgment.

He tried to explain to her what had happened—as much as he was able to remember—with all his routine fabrications thrown in. He was able to sense something new in her manner as she listened to him. There was a small fire in her eyes that he had never seen before, a hint of personal determination. Maybe it was just that she didn't seem to ask him so many questions. But this was something he was too tired to let himself worry about right then; it would come back to him later when he sobered up.

MARY GOES TO AL-ANON

Mary didn't start making dinner that evening. Instead, she ordered pizza to be delivered for the children. She didn't wake Nick, still asleep in his chair with his clothes on, the TV news droning. Her friend Alice had called and again asked her to go with her to a meeting of people who were concerned about drinking and drug use in their families. It was called Al-Anon, and it met once a week, on Monday evenings, at a church nearby. Alice had been after her to go to this meeting for months.

Mary had read the literature Alice gave her about Al-Anon. She imagined that her own situation might someday get as bad as these stories, but her husband hadn't hit her, he hadn't lost his job, and he hadn't had health problems. She was about to say to herself that he hadn't been arrested, but of course he had been, several times. In any event, she didn't think that talking with other sad sacks could help her much with her own situation. Today, though, she was desperate. She was worn out, at her wits' end. And Alice had called again. Today, she just didn't feel up to fighting it any longer, and she told Alice she would give Al-Anon a try.

To tell the truth, Mary wasn't much impressed by the first meeting she attended. She worried about being recognized. She felt out of place. But she did begin to understand that this was a place where serious people were dealing seriously with something that was a very big problem in her own life. Maybe she was able to quit making comparisons. Maybe she began to see the similarities between her own story and the stories others had to tell. She hung in there.

Mary wasn't at all sure about how Al-Anon helps people. She wasn't at all sure it was helping her. But going to these weekly meetings began to be a comfortable part of her life, and she looked forward to them. Nick taunted her about it, said it was an embarrassment to the family. "What makes you think someone has a problem around here?" he said. It was astonishing to her that she didn't have to spill her private life to the group. She hadn't even mentioned Nick's name, hardly mentioned his drinking, and yet she was beginning to feel more confident about herself and still hopeful that something would begin to work for her and Nick. Alice said the comfort Mary felt was "Al-Anon magic." But it all felt so ordinary, so normal. Mary realized that she felt a measure of relaxation she hadn't even known she was missing.

Mary was surprised to see people at the meetings who she would never have supposed had family alcohol and drug problems. She enjoyed the companionship of people who understood the pain and the fear that had built up in her over the years, and who also understood how she could stand by her husband through it all. She was glad to find she had so much in common with everyone else there.

HOW AL-ANON WORKS

People who stay with Al-Anon long enough to become comfortable, even if they don't know how the program works, will hear enough stories of other people to realize that their own stories are similar. As they finally begin to tell their own stories, they will hear the understanding responses of others. Through the process of talking and listening, a kind of reality checking begins to operate.

They see themselves as they listen to others who have made compromises in order to maintain peace in an alcoholic household. They hear others who have also spent sleepless nights waiting up for spouses who were out drinking or using drugs, and others who have sacrificed to make ends meet while they supported the alcohol and drug habits of someone they love. They hear others who have slammed doors, thrown dishes at the wall, and screamed in the night. They hear others who have

blindly hoped for improvement in situations that
always just get worse.

By comparing notes with others, people at Al-
Anon meetings learn to be objective about their
own situations. They learn to separate their real
fears from their imagined ones. They learn, slowly,
to recognize rationalizations they have invented to
maintain peace. They begin to see how they have
strayed away from the normal in the ways they've
been living their lives. They begin to reconnect
with their own normal expectations, if they ever
did have them. And they learn about what normal
expectations are, if they don't already know.

In another aspect of the reality-checking process,
Al-Anon helps people to see that alcoholism and addiction are not the fault of loved ones. A woman
like Mary can come to realize in a fresh new way
that she isn't responsible for her husband being an
alcoholic. She may already know this—such women
are often mature and sensible people and have seen
a lot of life—and yet the thought keeps persisting,
in some perverse way, that her husband wouldn't
drink if she were better, somehow, or different, in
some way. It is something that is hard for many
women like Mary to get out of their heads. It's just
as hard for children. And just as hard for the husbands of addicted women. Even though they all
may know better.

The most difficult lesson that Al-Anon has to
teach, however, is something that everyone learns
in the school of hard knocks that life with an alcoholic or an addict is. It's something that's repeated

in one story after another at almost every Al-Anon meeting. This lesson is that it is particularly difficult for a spouse or other close loved one to demand that someone quit drinking and make it stick, make it happen that way. Do alcoholics and addicts instinctively understand that deep bonds of affection seriously compromise the confrontational powers of their loved ones? That the deeper the bonds are, the more easily the power is compromised?

With problems like alcoholism, families become emotional survival systems as they try to get on with life, cure the problem, ignore it, live with it, all the while pretending it never happened. They adopt rigidly repetitive patterns of reactive behavior that simply maintain their problems.

Some family therapists believe they can best help families by giving them comfort, information, and understanding, and then by offering them special training in how to cope with crises. A goal for many therapists is to help families stay as calm as possible in the face of whatever the provocations of the troubled souls among them. In an informal way, Al-Anon meetings use similar methods to achieve similar goals.

HOW AL-ANON WAS CHANGING MARY

Mary would go after Nick with the challenging question, "If you loved me, you would quit drinking, wouldn't you?" First, Nick would deny that her premise was valid, and then he would turn away from the question. Often, it was the last exchange between them before another round of drinking. Over and over again, Mary's Al-Anon group assured her that she couldn't browbeat Nick into changing his drinking habits. The bitter truth is that anxiety about someone else's drinking and drug use just promotes more drinking and drug use. There's no getting around that hard rule, a rule that seems to be related to a basic human characteristic that I earlier referred to as insistence-resistance.

For years Mary had kept a personal journal. She wrote in it every day, and the very act of keeping it up-to-date was a source of comfort to her. In the past, when things were going badly with Nick, she would lose her objectivity, and her interest in the journal would fade at these times. Now, the Al-Anon meetings and what she was learning there—not only about alcoholism but also about herself—began to be a major subject in the journal.

"Nick is still drinking," she recorded.

> "He's more careful about what he docs, but getting arrested in Detroit is already part of the past. It's almost as if the whole thing never happened. Can he see that I'm beginning to understand all this a little better, that I'm getting more realistic about what's happening to us? And that I love him still? Can he tell I'm not being so

suspicious and resentful? Can he see that I'm trying hard not to fight with him about drinking? Does he see that I'm different? I wonder if he does."

Mary was learning something very important, something that freed her to think even more clearly about what was happening to her family and about what she could do about it: she was beginning to know that she could be realistic about Nick's drinking and that she could still love him just the same. Realizing that being realistic did not mean needing to hate him was a wonderfully freeing new awareness for her.

Later, she wrote,

"I know he put a bottle of vodka on the high shelf in the garage, but I'm not going to ask him about it. I don't want to have my own kind of relapse at this stage of the game. That bottle is his problem to deal with, not mine!"

Mary thought about this for a few moments, tapping her pencil on the desk, and then began writing again in her journal,

"I could put a ladder up and reach the bottle, empty it on the ground, and throw the damn thing in the trash. But Nick will know that I've done that, and he'll be angry and ashamed, and we'll fight about it.

And he'll just go out and buy another bottle anyway. So, what will I have proved?"

By thinking over the whole situation and not reacting immediately, Mary's practicing what Al-Anon calls "detachment." Writing in her journal—and thinking about what she will say at her Al-Anon meeting—helps her to look at the larger picture, to consider all of her other options. She left the bottle on the shelf.

A month later, as part of a longer entry, Mary wrote,

> "I'm not going to ask him to explain where he's been when he comes home late. But this is so damned hard for me. It's almost driving me crazy! What if he's in a car wreck tonight? And me doing nothing to stop it? But then, what could I do to stop it anyway? Damn! I need my meeting!"

Mary hardly knew how to explain what "needing a meeting" meant, but she knew it wasn't just leaning on other people. "You're my reality check," she'd said recently to the group. And that seemed right to her.

NICK'S TURNING POINT

For several months after the Detroit episode, Nick cleaned up his act. He knew that his boss was on to his drinking. He didn't know how much more Mary would put up with, and he didn't even want to think about this. She had changed since she had begun going to those Al-Anon meetings. He felt like hell when he had hangovers, and it was hard for him to concentrate on his work. As a result, he was trying hard to control when he drank and how much he drank.

But then, little by little, he began to fall back into his old patterns. By this time, Nick had become an insightful drunk: someone who really does know, who agonizes endlessly over the fact that he drinks too much, but who continues to drink anyway. It's a terrible thing to know about yourself, and it's a desperate way to live your life. One spring night he came home drunk again sometime after 1:00 A.M. He sat in the car in the driveway and smoked a cigarette. He couldn't make his eyes focus quite right. He was trying to pull himself together again, and he was thinking about what he would say to Mary.

At that odd moment of drunken reflection, it occurred to him that Mary hadn't been asking him much about drinking. He walked up the steps and let himself in, ready to explain to her that he had had to work late. But the lights were out, and Mary wasn't waiting. When he walked upstairs, he found her there, sound asleep in bed! As he tried to get himself ready for bed without waking her up, he felt deeply frightened.

Nick thought often about this night later on, when he was in a treatment center. He realized it marked a turning point in his relationship with Mary. He realized that this was when she began to pull herself together. She began to let him know she expected him to behave like an adult, not like another child that she had to take care of. "Mom" hadn't waited up for him to come home.

Two months later, Nick was involved in what was almost a repetition of the earlier Detroit incident that had urged Mary to go to Al-Anon. This time, Mary didn't cover for him. She didn't call his office for him. When Nick's boss called the house, she told him where Nick was.

Still later, while he was a patient in an alcoholism rehabilitation program, Nick recalled how threatened he had felt by the sleeping Mary—not by what she said or did, but by what she no longer said and did. That was the night, when she was detached enough to get a good night's sleep, that she officially gave his drinking problems back to him.

HITTING BOTTOM

At this particular time in our history, our culture is lifting the "bottom" so that when the alcoholic hits it, the tumble doesn't need to be so hard. As in Nick and Mary's story, education about alcoholism and other drug addictions, and about the resources that are available for treatment and care, have helped many people to begin living sober and clean lives before they have lost everything. It is much more common now than it once was to find people who have diagnosed themselves before they lose their jobs, before their families turn away from them, before they suffer health problems. There are more people now who have said to themselves that they are "sick and tired of being sick and tired" and have sobered up before too much damage is done.

Old-timers in Alcoholics Anonymous often said that an alcoholic had to "hit bottom" before any progress could be made toward sobriety. The mythology was that an alcoholic who still owned a wristwatch that he hadn't pawned yet, or who could still afford to drive his own car, was probably not far enough down-and-out to join AA and stay sober. Today, a whole different attitude prevails. People are seeking help at younger ages from therapists, mental health agencies, and treatment centers—and often they're driving to AA meetings in their own cars.

TYPES OF INTERVENTION

Often, alcoholism is diagnosed after someone's work is affected by problem drinking and his or her job is threatened. Employers are usually able to be more objective about problem drinking than family members are; employers can assess someone's impaired functioning in terms of lost time at work, decreased productivity, ineffectiveness, and so forth. Employee assistance programs have enjoyed a high level of success with encouraging one group of people—middle-aged men—to get help. This group of people seems to be more influenced by the real threat of losing their jobs than by the possibility of losing their long-suffering families. Traditionally, loss of job meant loss of supply of alcohol and other drugs.

There are quite a few people who are forced to assess their drinking problems when they are arrested for driving while intoxicated. One of the most common of all intervention techniques is the DWI, which serves as an eye-opener to many people. Still others are forced to make realistic diagnoses of their drinking when they're faced with physical health problems and their physicians are wise enough to make the connection, in spite of patients' protestations.

For individual families, a commonly discussed technique for helping someone who has crossed the line into addiction is called the structured intervention. Intervention has come to mean an all-out battle plan, complete with significant friends, relatives, and business associates, any and all therapists with an interest in the matter, a reservation at an out-of-state treatment center, and an airline ticket for a flight that evening. Mary, as are many people, was not up to this. However, as she illustrated, there are ways to intervene that are not simply frontal attacks. It's another kind of intervention, an intervention that's consistent with the principles of Al-Anon, and with the new family-systems thinking mentioned earlier. Let me explain.

AN AWFUL PREDICTABILITY

Families living with alcoholism tend to establish patterns of behavior, and they repeat these patterns over and over. You might say that life assumes an awful sort of predictability—although every separate drinking episode may be a variation on the theme, and therefore there's an element of unpredictability, too. Anxious families usually become very sensitive to one another; they may take things too personally, and little things become as important as big ones. They overreact to one another. Families coping with addiction tend to be people who seem to require more drama in life than most other people do, perhaps because they have accustomed themselves to lives of building tensions, explosive climaxes, and depressing finales.

Anxious family members who are coping with addiction sometimes pretend to ignore the problem. They will act tough and lock the door and say that the addict has to solve his or her own problem. This approach is easiest to take when it's obvious that someone else is confronting the problem, often a spouse or another relative or friend. Even so, people taking the tough-love approach may find that they lie awake in the early morning hours waiting for a knock at the door.

Or, conversely, some family members will become overly preoccupied with protecting the addict, pleading and reasoning, trying to contain the problem, covering up, mending the damage, bandaging the wounds, paying the bills, soliciting promises. A client came to Hazelden several years ago who each night had been setting a pocket alarm clock to alert himself, in New York, to place a telephone call to his sister in Paris to wake her up in the morning to go to work. The sister was a recovering alcoholic who would periodically experience very dramatic relapses. Her regular periods of sobriety, which were followed predictably by self-destructive binges, had gone on for ten years.

Every binge was by now as routine as a fire drill: the brother and his legal and medical team members on two continents all went to their stations on cue. The sister in Paris knew they could always be counted on to intervene in reaction to her drinking. She didn't want to know this. No one involved in the game wanted to admit that they knew the routine.

BREAKING THE ROUTINE

Here's another example: Ellen is a thirty-five-year-old housewife and the mother of three small children. She's from a factory town in Ohio. Her husband, Bill, is a production worker in a manufacturing company. He has a good job with a future, and he is a good provider for the family. They've been married for ten years, and they love each other, and they look like a perfect old-fashioned family—almost like a throwback to the 1950s.

That is, it looked this way until recently, when Ellen had to go to the hospital emergency room for treatment for a broken nose. Then it came out that there was a secret problem in this family. A social worker helped Ellen to face up to the fact that Bill had gotten drunk in a bar every Friday evening on payday for months—maybe for years, she couldn't remember—and that he had verbally and physically abused her every Friday night in their bedroom. Ellen had a hard time admitting this. The abuse had been bad for her before, but she had gotten used to it. Her method of coping? Every Friday morning, she went downstairs to the deep freeze and made some ice packs for her own face, to prepare herself for the predictable evening attack.

Typically, Bill would wake up on Saturday filled with remorse. He would spend the weekend sober, trying to repair the damage. By Monday, things would be back to normal again. They did not keep liquor in their house, and Bill never drank on any day except Friday.

Ellen had a wise social worker. She didn't start by helping Ellen figure out what to do about this once-a-week monster that her husband became. Instead, she encouraged Ellen to take a long look at the patterns of interaction in her relationship with her husband. Patiently, over a period of weeks, she won Ellen's trust. As Ellen reviewed the recent past—honestly, without deceiving herself—the first thing she was able to realize was that the Friday beatings had gone on for months, and, yes, for a couple of years. It was hard for her to look at this. She had been telling herself all this time that the beatings were an aberration—not a regular part of their life.

Then, with some further coaching, she began to realize that she had come to expect to be abused and beaten every Friday, and that she had regularly made the ice packs for herself. This was a very difficult realization, something that she found hard to let sink in. She felt like a crazy person. She felt humiliated. Her new ally, the social worker, comforted her with assurances that this was the way it sometimes went when people were trying to cope with alcoholism. She urged Ellen to attend an Al-Anon meeting, where she would meet others who understood what had happened to her, who understood how she had reacted, who could assure her that she wasn't crazy.

Finally, Ellen was able to take a good look at how willing she was, after every episode was over, to pretend that nothing had happened. She dearly wanted Bill to be a different person. She wanted him to change. She too readily accepted his tearful apologies and his promises to quit drinking, because she loved him. And she continued to hope, even as their dangerous game went on, that he would change.

Bill did not quit drinking on Friday afternoons, but he was on his good behavior for the next few weeks because the social worker was now involved. This gave Ellen and the worker some time to figure out a strategy.

With the social worker along, Ellen took Bill to the basement on a Saturday morning and showed him how she had made the ice packs for her own face, and she told him she wasn't going to do that any longer. Then she convened a house meeting, with the social worker present again, and asked the three children to tell Bill what they knew about his Friday night drinking. Finally, because Bill's mother was a pretty good pal of Ellen's, Ellen told her about the broken nose, the ice packs, and the meeting with the children. She invited her mother-in-law to come to their house every Friday evening, to become a regular part of their Friday schedule.

The social worker who told me this story said there was peace and quiet in this household through the following winter. Bill got a promotion at work, and the family moved to California. She didn't know if Bill quit drinking altogether, but Ellen became a new person. A significant intervention took place in this case, even though Ellen didn't insist that Bill stop drinking. Some people wouldn't even recognize this as an "intervention," but it was. And notice, it took some time. It was not a single melodramatic event.

There are many reasons why people become addicted to alcohol and other drugs. The story of Ben and Sarah in the next chapter illustrates this.

CHAPTER THREE

Why Do Some People
Become Addicted
to Drugs and Alcohol?

BEN

A light autumn rain is falling. Ben curses the slow traffic at the light. He swings his car onto the ramp, downshifts to pick up speed, and enters the freeway with a flying start, heading north from Des Moines to Saint Paul—and Sarah. No stoplights the whole way, he thinks to himself, I'll be there by 3:00, easy.

Ben is a forty-year-old African-American businessman. He was born in South Chicago and grew up there in a large family, in the fear and oppression—and the secure enclosure—of the ghetto. After a Marine Corps tour of duty in Vietnam, he went to the University of Iowa on the GI Bill. His successes in life, both in the military and at the university, gave him a sense of self-confidence. He decided to stay in Iowa on a cocky whim: maybe he wanted to demand his civil rights in this white-bread territory.

He borrowed money and started a small high-tech manufacturing operation in Des Moines. The business climate was strong there at the time, and he felt welcome in the community. Ben was confident that he could make it, but he also knew what he was up against as a black businessman. He found a corner of the marketplace in which he neither asked nor gave quarter.

As for the social life of a black in this largely white community, he knows that he's welcome—in a certain way. He still hasn't gotten used to self-conscious, well-intentioned WASP attitudes, somehow worse than honest bigotry. But Des Moines is home for him now—now that he's established in business there, now that he has met Sarah, an African-American social worker he has fallen in love with. He and Sarah lived together for two years. They were making plans to marry until the day three months ago when she overdosed on a combination of alcohol and tranquilizers and wound up in the hospital.

Ben is crazy about Sarah, and he's crazy now to see her again. Now that she's in treatment, he wonders if he will still have a place in her new life. He wonders if he will lose her. That's one part of what is going on with Ben. That's his heart speaking. They've talked often on the phone, but they haven't been together since she left for the treatment center in Saint Paul over two months ago.

Sometime around 3:00, he repeats to himself. Maybe I'll go to the hotel first and call. What will she say? How will she look? What will she think about us, now that she's been in treatment? How's it going to be? Was it something I was doing wrong? "Damn it!" he cries out to no one but himself.

It's a downpour now, and the windshield wipers slap back and forth. Ben tries to concentrate on the road, but his thoughts wander. There's another aspect of his relationship with Sarah. He is angry in some vague way that he can't define. The depth of his feelings for her frightens him. He realizes now that Sarah has a big problem that she has to cope with herself. He believes that he can't really count on her now, in the way that he once did. Before he met Sarah, his life was given to the development of his company. He could cope with business problems. And he always tried to keep his social life well within a manageable range. His relationship with Sarah is something else. There's really no telling what's ahead, and he doesn't like that.

Ben's company manufactures certain components for computers used in farm equipment. Over the years, he has trained six new production staff for a total of twelve. He has bought or designed and built all the equipment they use. The company has finally come out of the red. He has paid off the last of his loans. At the same time, Ben knows that elements of his manufacturing operation are becoming obsolete.

He's known this for several months, but he's been

so worried about Sarah that he hasn't been thinking clearly. As well as being the CEO, Ben is also the whole research and development department for this one-horse outfit. His feelings for Sarah crowd in on him now. How can he run his business when he can't get her off his mind? And how can he even be there for her when he's so preoccupied with the business?

Suddenly he's feeling resentful—and confused. How can you resent someone you love? Why doesn't she get past this problem so they can get married? Why is she an addict? How could she have let this happen to her? If he could just drop everything and take care of her, what could he do for her? Sarah's counselor says that her addiction is a problem that she'll have to handle herself. What the hell is he talking about? The blast of a truck's air horn warns him that he's drifting out of his lane.

SARAH

Sarah stretches and rolls over on her back when the alarm sounds off. Head still under the covers, she reaches out for the clock. She turns off the alarm and finds her cigarettes and lighter, almost in one motion. Now she pulls herself up to sit cross-legged in the middle of the bed. She lights a cigarette and inhales deeply. And she begins to think about the day—and about the weekend ahead, with Ben. The weather looks terrible, she says to herself. I'll bet he left early to be here when I finish work this afternoon. Ben is always there for me. Why is he always so damned thoughtful? Why do I need him so much?

It's the end of Sarah's third week in a Saint Paul halfway house. She spent a month in a treatment program, then decided she wasn't ready to go back to her job as a social worker at a mental-health clinic in Des Moines. She still doesn't know how to plan her own future. All she knows is that she wants to be careful, that she doesn't want to proceed impulsively. She finds herself thinking about her relationships with others and analyzing behaviors and conversations. She has become so self-conscious that it's difficult for her to be spontaneous about anything.

She wants to have the personal satisfaction that her professional career once gave her, but she doesn't even trust herself right now, and why should anyone else believe in her? A mental-health counselor who overdosed and wound up in a treatment center as a patient? An addicted social worker who's been living in a halfway house on her way up the career ladder? No way! she thinks to herself.

She loves Ben, and she wants him to come to her now and hold her and comfort her. These feelings are all mixed up with the guilt she feels about the misery she has already caused him. And she hasn't even told him yet about her sexual activity while they were living together. Could this confession cause more harm than good? Right now it seems that it might. She thinks she wants to be married to Ben. She thinks that she wants to have children. But she's not certain of anything. She even tells herself she doesn't deserve that kind of happiness. It would be easier, she thinks sometimes, to leave Ben, to leave Des Moines and her family, and to make a fresh start in a new place with people who don't care about her past.

At this point in her recovery, she thinks about sobriety as a life-or-death matter. She is staying sober—one day at a time. She says to herself that if nothing else is going right for her, at least she has her sobriety. She thanks God for that, but she also gives herself some of the credit. So, every day now her sobriety gives her something to be grateful for. It is something that helps to bolster her self-confidence. Her sobriety is a very important thing to her, maybe the most important thing in her life right now.

But she's terrified that she won't be able to stay sober. She wonders if her relationship with Ben is dangerous for her at this time when she knows she is very vulnerable. Her thoughts keep wandering back to all the regrets she feels about the past. Then they jump far out ahead to speculate about what looks like a very uncertain future.

And on this rainy autumn morning, she's glad that she's in a halfway house, safe and sound, clean and sober, with some time to figure out her life. In this room, she feels the kind of security she felt in her own room in her childhood home. And she feels free from the need to make decisions. She can hardly wait for Ben to get here—and she wishes that he weren't coming at all. Both these thoughts cross her mind and make her feel crazy. And feeling crazy reminds her of being high. And being high is exactly what terrifies her the most. "Damn!"

EXPECTATIONS VS. REALITY

In many respects, Ben and Sarah are a typical upwardly mobile middle-class couple. They come from families that have set high standards for themselves, they're bright and well-educated, and they expect to succeed in life. They also face the difficult decisions that often trouble people in their generation when they decide to marry.

Many young people who now make their careers the central focus of their lives postpone marriage until they have achieved certain career goals. Through the years, they manage to learn how to live alone, or in temporary relationships, with a degree of contentment. Learning about the joys and sacrifices involved in living a committed life with another person can be a difficult struggle.

Often, for young middle-aged people, it's no longer a matter of blindly falling in love; they know too much about life. More maturity often means more anguished analysis of relationships and less joyous spontaneity. All too often, people like this find themselves bogged down in an endless search for the perfect relationship.

Even when they are realistic enough to make necessary compromises, they have to learn how to negotiate such matters as who is going to change what personal career goals in order to make the marriage work? Who will have to do what in order to maintain the standard of living they have enjoyed? Maybe they decide to go off in a new direction with their lives. Is it or isn't it possible to include children in their plans? As youth begins to give way to middle age, and people like these are struggling with vitally important decisions, they are reminded again and again that the clock is ticking.

BEN'S FAMILY

Ben came from a strong family, working-class parents, a half-dozen brothers and sisters. From childhood on, it just wasn't in him to become an addict. He grew up smart and tough in the midst of urban poverty and crime and alcohol and drug abuse—a homeboy who aspired to a career in business. He had the street knowledge and the muscle it took to succeed in the neighborhood, but he went off in another direction, enlisting in the Marines and spending the last few months of the war in Vietnam.

Ben learned so much at home about the joys of

family life that he grew up with a healthy optimism. He believed that if you take responsibility for your life, it's possible to make some things work out the way you want them to. He has seen how alcoholism and addiction hurt people—in his Chicago neighborhood, during his tour in Vietnam, at his university, and, more recently, as a business executive. In his own view of the world, blacks can make it, but they have an uphill struggle even if they don't mess themselves up with alcohol and drug problems.

SARAH'S FAMILY

Sarah grew up in a middle-class family, with a different set of expectations than Ben had. Like Ben, she had the support of a solid family background. She also had self-confidence that came from her own successes in life. While growing up, she had endured more day-to-day racial prejudice in her integrated Des Moines neighborhood than Ben experienced in the ghetto. Paradoxically, integration promised more than it delivered to many people like Sarah who lived in basically progressive communities, places where integration actually made some headway, where the battle for equal rights was joined.

As blacks in the Midwest, Ben and Sarah must contend with their racial identity every day—in

their personal lives and in their social and professional relationships with others. Although they
both have middle-class jobs, middle-class standards
of life, they are reminded every day, in one way or
another, of their minority status. Even for people
like Ben and Sarah who are beating the odds, racial inequality is a burden that complicates their
lives. It figures in how they both perceive Sarah's
alcohol and drug problems and how they cope with
them.

Sarah and Ben had faced all these difficult questions during the years they had been together.
They faced them again in long late-night telephone
conversations when Sarah was in Saint Paul.
Somehow, they always returned to the overriding
matter of Sarah's addiction and her recovery program, the major issue in their lives, one that complicated every plan they tried to make.

WHY DO SOME PEOPLE BECOME ADDICTED?

Sarah was thirty when she and Ben met. She
was a presenter at a seminar on human relations
that her agency conducted for a group of small
businesses. Ben was a fascinated member of her
audience. They had lunch together, and they fell in
love. A year later, they were living in Ben's apartment, planning a future together. Before another
year passed, Sarah had been arrested once for
DWI, she had overdosed on prescription drugs, and

she had wound up in a treatment center—and then a halfway house. And now Ben wonders why it all happened. Why had Sarah become an alcoholic, an addict? And why couldn't she pull herself together and be finished with that problem?

During the time after Sarah's overdose and hospitalization, while she was in treatment, Ben turned himself into an expert on the subject of addiction. He talked to a counselor at the local referral and information center. He read everything he could find about addiction and treatment. He went back to the family therapist that he and Sarah had seen briefly, hoping to find answers. He wanted to understand what had happened to Sarah. He wanted to know what she was going through now.

There isn't a simple answer, as Ben discovered, to the question of why a small percentage of the population become addicts and alcoholics while most people do not. In this country, chemical dependency occurs among males and females—the old and the young, the rich and the poor—in such a thoroughly democratic way that there is no typical chemically dependent person, no typical family with concerns about chemical dependency.

We do understand some things about alcoholism and addiction to other drugs, but much of the story is still mysterious. The experts agree that very probably there is a genetic element involved. Addicts and alcoholics probably share an inherited propensity for harmful dependence on psychoactive substances. Studies of identical twins, for example, who have grown up separated from one another, in quite different environments, reveal that the twins have similar rates of addiction to alcohol and other drugs.

Some people seem to be more vulnerable to addiction than others are. It seems to be related to how their bodies metabolize mood-altering chemicals. There was no alcoholism in Sarah's immediate family, as far as Ben could discover. That didn't rule out the possibility of genetic vulnerability, however. Maybe the vulnerability was there, but Sarah's near relatives weren't tempted to abuse alcohol or other drugs.

Tolerance

One aspect of the genetic argument has to do with tolerance. We've all heard about people who can "drink you under the table," or people with very expensive drug habits. You might think that those who can drink a lot and still appear to be sober, or those who need a lot of drugs to get high, are the ones who will avoid becoming addicted. Quite the opposite: you have to drink a lot to become an alcoholic; you have to use a lot of drugs to become an addict.

Tolerance is really one of the most obvious symptoms of the problem. People with normal tolerance levels can't handle very much of the disorientation of being high. They get sick. Their bodies just won't let them become addicts. Ben always thought that only a small amount of alcohol could get Sarah into a lot of trouble. He never did realize how much medication she was taking secretly.

But there's more to it than genetics. People are not destined to become addicted in the way that they might be genetically destined to be left-handed, bald, or tall. Heredity is only one of a number of factors that figure in the causes for addiction.

Social Environment

The social environment is another important factor. There is something, after all, to the idea that people use drugs and alcohol in ways that are influenced by peer pressure. Again, as in the case for genetics, we have to realize that peer pressure is only a part of the picture; not everyone succumbs. Peer pressure is an influencing factor somehow in all of our lives, not only in the lives of schoolchildren. Most of us tend to follow the fashions of our peers right on through to the blue hair and the pastel polyesters. In communities that are intolerant of intoxication, chances are that problems with intoxication will be less evident than in communities that offer easy access to alcohol.

Ben and Sarah lived an active social life, and some drinking was involved. However, all across the country people's drinking habits have been influenced significantly by health consciousness and temperance. Ben and Sarah's thoroughly up-to-date friends were not "swingers." None of them abused prescription drugs; no one used illegal drugs. A lot

of their friends, in fact, were health buffs who ate
lots of carrots and drank mineral water at parties.
Some others were recovering people who were abstinent. Sarah had to disguise the extent of her
drinking, usually, even among their social friends.

Family Environment

Another important aspect of the problem is family environment. The examples that family members set for one another, the unwritten rules that
they obey about drugs and alcohol, help to shape
the attitudes of children. Most of us wind up with
many of the same attitudes about alcohol and
drugs that our parents had, or else we try hard to
defy these rules. In either case, the family manages
to prevail. One way or another, our families influence our behavior.

Sarah's family, like Ben's own family, was intolerant of alcoholic drinking, not to mention the misuse
of drugs. Illegal drugs were out of the question altogether. So Sarah was rebelling against strong
family norms in this respect. Her parents were not
only frightened when she overdosed, they were bro-
kenhearted.

Denial That a Problem Exists

Both Sarah and Ben knew that Sarah was stoned
every now and then, but they never talked about it.
When she was arrested and went to court, Ben was
completely astonished. He had managed to deny to

himself the fairly obvious fact that Sarah was abusing alcohol and drugs. It didn't seem to him that she drank so very much. In fact, she didn't need to drink a lot to be stoned, because secretly she was on a maintenance high of tranquilizers and amphetamines—with prescriptions from several different doctors.

Sarah was able to persuade Ben that she was being treated unfairly by the police, and she won him over. People who are devoted to one another can do this sort of thing. To admit to themselves, to one another, and to the outside world that they have a serious problem like addiction is threatening to couples who are trying to build a relationship. To further confuse the issue, Ben quietly enjoyed the fact that Sarah needed him sometimes to take care of her. He just liked to feel that he was needed.

Eventually, Ben did begin to recognize that Sarah just wasn't being herself. But even if he did suspect that she was suffering from alcohol and drug abuse, he couldn't admit this. To see Sarah as addicted would mean to him that she was weak and that she was falling apart. For months, he attributed her changed behavior to the stresses of her job and to problems they were having as a couple. At the same time, he characteristically refused to give her much sympathy. This lack of sympathy on his part, not an alcohol- or drug-related incident, was what led to the first serious rift between them. It was an unfeeling confrontation, during which Ben accused Sarah of feeling sorry for herself and gave her a lecture on this topic.

Sarah was furious. She broke off the relationship and moved out of Ben's place to her old room in her parents' house. After a few weeks, during which both of them were miserable, they made up and Sarah agreed to live with Ben again—if he would go with her to a family therapist. Through three counseling sessions in the next three weeks, no mention was ever made by either of them of Sarah's alcohol and drug use.

That was a subject neither of them wanted to talk about, each for very different reasons. This kind of collaboration in the denial of a pretty obvious problem usually has a history. It is woven into the texture of the relationship. And it wasn't until the evening that Ben came home late from the office and found Sarah lying comatose on the floor in the bedroom that the two of them were forced to face up to the problem.

About Family Attitudes on Alcohol and Drugs

Family rules regarding alcohol and drugs are especially important today in this country, because we do not have well-established cultural norms for the use of these mood-altering substances, and there are few social codes that we can all agree on. Our melting-pot culture has many different opinions about alcohol and other drugs and how they should be used. Young people may be confused by the different messages coming from the liquor industry and from public-health educators.

Laws that govern the availability of alcohol vary

from one state to another, from one county to another within states. Penalties for public intoxication are very strictly enforced in some communities and more or less ignored in others. This is why the family's rules about alcohol and other drugs become so important.

Sarah is a good example of a person who rebelled against the family rules and went her own way, though her family had consistent and reasonable standards and values about alcohol and drug use. Even if the family rules aren't a sure means of prevention, they're important, given the mixed messages that result from our cultural confusion.

Think how risky the situation is for children in families with one parent who approves of alcohol and the other parent who is critical and abstinent. How do these children figure out how to behave around alcohol and drugs? Children like this are certain to be more vulnerable to the misuse of alcohol and drugs than are children who grow up with well-defined codes of conduct.

Psychological Makeup

Still another reason that some people become addicted and others don't has to do with the psychological makeup of the individual. Addictive behavior is the harmful acting out of thoroughly human impulses, "the devices and desires of our own hearts," as *The Book of Common Prayer* puts it. Conventional wisdom tells us that some people are blessed with more inner strength than others have. It would seem that some of us are psychologically invulnerable to addictions, and that others of us, maybe even most of us, are quite vulnerable.

As Sarah gradually succumbed to alcoholism and drug abuse, her inner strength began to fail her. She began to see herself as a victim, an attitude that is all too typical among practicing addicts and alcoholics. She let herself use racial prejudice as an explanation for her unhappiness and as a justification for her behavior. This victim attitude was something that Sarah was really unable to realize. She overslept and missed appointments with clients and then complained of being hassled at work. She blamed the cops for her DWI arrest. She neglected to pay credit card bills and then complained that Visa and MasterCard were unfair to her.

At first, Ben tried to be sympathetic, though it ran against his grain somehow. He wondered, Did she drink because she was under a lot of stress? Or was her life so stressful because she was drinking too much? He didn't even know about the prescription drugs. He wanted to believe her. He wanted to support her. But her erratic behavior and her excuses and her blaming of others began to take their toll on their relationship.

Ben's glass may have been mostly empty during his childhood, but he grew up expecting that. He was imbued from the beginning with a strong sense of racial pride. Sarah's family was the only black family on their block, one of only a few in a neighborhood that thought of itself as being enlightened.

Sarah was forever finding that her glass was half-empty, forever expecting it to be full.

All through life, either Sarah was feeling confident about her achievements, in spite of racial prejudice, or else she was feeling trapped and oppressed by prejudice. She was driven by some deep and powerful urges to succeed in her profession. She genuinely wanted to help other people; she also wanted to make her own mark. Her expectations often ran far enough ahead of her performance to keep her feeling unhappy.

People who are comfortable about themselves seem to be less prone to addictive disorders than those who require a lot of outside reinforcement. These are people who have a good level of self-respect, who recognize their own strengths as well as their shortcomings. They listen to and respond to others, but they aren't dependent on the approval of others. They feel able to deal with most situations that come their way, and they can accept their limitations. They can enjoy simple everyday pleasures, and they can accept disappointments.

On the other hand, people with low levels of self-confidence, who depend heavily on others for their good feelings about themselves, are at a higher level of risk of becoming addicted to alcohol and drugs. They need the good feelings that these substances produce. People who are psychologically vulnerable to becoming addicts include those who are particularly serious about themselves, who are very sensitive to others, who are bowled over by disappointments.

They are apt to be as critical and intolerant of others as they are of themselves. They may find it difficult to trust and to like others. They either worry too much about others, or they ignore others and fail to consider their interests.

They are people who find it difficult to play any significant part in shaping their own environment, people who are unable to set realistic goals for themselves, people who are unable to plan and follow through to the achievement of their goals. They're the ones who cannot accept responsibility for things that happen to them, who see themselves instead as the victims of circumstances that are beyond their control.

Human Nature

Efforts have been made by scientists to discover an accurate psychological portrait of the addict. Yet it's very difficult to make useful generalizations about such a thoroughly human problem. Addiction doesn't lend itself well to scientific description. In any event, the psychological profile is only part of the total problem.

There is another thought that deserves special consideration. As we attempt to be scientific about predicting addiction and diagnosing it, we have to recognize that it's human nature to fool the experts. There surely are people out there who are wending their way through this vale of tears with no drug and alcohol problems, in spite of having all of the indicators for addiction—including an inherited physical vulnerability to alcohol and drug abuse; family, work, and social environments where alcohol and other drugs are available and where intoxication is encouraged; and personal, emotional, spiritual, and psychological fragility. All these factors are parts of a mix that is often associated with addiction, but they are only indicators, they are not accurate predictors of addiction.

It all boils down to the fact that when you have an addict, you have just another frail human being, nothing more special than that, and nothing less special. A typical alcoholic or addict is simply a typical person—a typical person who has wandered away from the campfire while searching for wildflowers or snipes or the ultimate meaning of life, and who just can't find the way back.

One of the ways Ben can cope with Sarah's addiction is through detachment. We can all learn how to care for ourselves using this technique discussed in the next chapter.

CHAPTER FOUR

Detachment:
A Special Kind of Caring

Is drug addiction a disease? Is alcoholism a disease? It could be that this is a false question. Maybe the real question is, Are you willing to look at alcoholism or drug addiction as a disease? Or do you know of a better way to approach these problems? Ben was still thinking that one over.

From his research and his long talks with Sarah, Ben was beginning to get some understanding of the treatment program and the halfway house. He knew they were helping Sarah. He could hear a new sense of confidence in her voice when they talked on the phone. However, though he never said this to Sarah, he couldn't help feeling she could pull herself together on her own, if she would only do it—without all the special care she was getting.

He was still angry and disappointed in her for

getting into this predicament. He was upset with himself for falling in love with an addict. He didn't want to blame her, but he did blame her nevertheless. Ben was someone who succeeded all his life by using good judgment. In spite of all that he had learned so far about addiction from the experts, his judgment told him that Sarah was a flawed person. He was afraid that her problems could drag them both down. His involvement with her was already a major problem for him; he wasn't able to think about the management of his company.

In spite of what his good judgment told him, his heart told him to try to work things out with Sarah. He loved her. He yearned for her. He needed her. He wanted to marry her. Maybe they could still make a life together. If he could only figure out why she had become an addict, he felt, maybe the two of them could lick this problem together.

THE SEARCH FOR ANSWERS

Ben was still caught in that fruitless search for answers, still trying to analyze the problem. He still believed locating the cause would give Sarah—and him—the cure. And so, instead of just loving Sarah, he worried about her.

More often than not, family members identify alcohol and drug problems before the problem person does. When it comes to understanding the complex process of recovery, however, recovering alcoholics

who have turned the corner are often able to lead
the way. This was the case with Sarah and Ben.

At dinner on their first evening together in Saint
Paul, Ben and Sarah talked mostly about the new
direction that her life was taking, her new confidence. They discussed her treatment program and
her halfway-house experiences, her plans. For the
first time, Ben's suffering revealed itself, too—how
much he cared for Sarah, as well as how angry he
was, how uncertain, and how fearful.

Ben wanted to take Sarah to the theater to cele-
brate their reunion. She talked him into going to
an Al-Anon meeting instead. Instead of debating
with him, she wanted him to hear about Al-Anon
from other people. She knew that if he would listen, others could help to ease his mind. She also
knew Ben well enough to see that he might have a
hard time listening, and an even harder time getting the message.

People like Ben use power, strength, and ability
to analyze situations. Then they figure out what all
the problems are and manage them through to
workable solutions. And then they move on to new
challenges. In short, Ben was one of those people
who are accustomed to winning through thought
and action. Al-Anon doesn't work that way.

To Sarah's great surprise, Ben stepped out of his
Captain of Industry mode and went to the meeting
with her, with no argument at all. The Al-Anon
speaker was a middle-aged white-haired woman
named Aggie whose husband had died of alcoholism. At this meeting, AA friends and relatives were

also invited to attend. As Ben sat with Sarah, he sensed that there was something genuine about all this, that these were people to be reckoned with. And he listened. And he learned. He even took notes as if he were at a business seminar.

WHY? WHY? WHY?

The speaker focused on three basic pointers for newcomers to Al-Anon. Her first subject was a warning that people don't make progress in coping with addictions until they can quit asking "Why?" This basic message of AA and Al-Anon came as a surprise to Ben. It caught his attention.

People who make it in AA are the ones who are able to accept responsibility for their drinking and drug abuse. The ones who are grateful for a chance to clean up their lives and then begin doing just that. In Al-Anon, it's the ones who quit making excuses for their loved ones who make it. They quit trying to figure out why their loved ones went the way they went. They quit blaming other people for their problems. They quit trying to analyze themselves and others. Alcoholics in AA and their friends and relatives in Al-Anon all take this same existential approach as they work a day at a time on their own recovery.

People in AA quit asking "why" because they know that one reason only leads to another reason. Creative people can think up whole new sets of reasons any day of the week. Why? Because the guys at the office expect you to drink. Because you don't want to offend the host at the party. Because you're anxious or because you're bored. Because your husband left you or because he's coming home. Because you're Irish. Or Greek. Or Scandinavian. All of these good valid reasons serve only to let you off the hook for your own behavior.

Al-Anon members—the husbands and wives, parents and children, lovers and friends of addicts—have the same obligation to quit asking "why." For all of these same reasons and for another big one as well: when these people look for reasons for their loved ones' addictive behaviors, they, too, can come up with all the excuses that addicts themselves find. If they continue to provide sympathy, they simply prolong the problems by failing to hold their loved ones accountable for responsible behavior.

But there's an additional heavy-duty reason for loved ones not to look for the reasons for addictive drinking and drug use. Too often they come up with the answer that it's their fault, that they've done something to cause the trouble. And the addict is all too often willing to concur in this reasoning and reinforce it by blaming loved ones. This is a major unfair cause of heartache among the family members, friends, and lovers of alcoholics and addicts.

Pulling your lives back together again, either in AA or in Al-Anon, means giving up all the Why? questions to ask, instead, a bunch of other questions: the Who? What? Where? When? and How? questions. These are the questions whose answers help you get to the heart of the matter. The answers help you to get honest with yourselves and others.

GETTING HONEST WITH YOURSELF

These questions emphasize the importance of total honesty about alcohol and other drugs. This goes for alcoholics and addicts as well as their loved ones. By the time you have identified your own or someone else's addiction, you know that you've been dishonest with yourself for a long time, over a whole history of episodes. That's just the way it is. To change things, it's essential to begin now to be honest, at least with yourself.

If you find yourself feeling that you need to hide or minimize someone's drinking or drug use, beware. You may be entering into a conspiracy that can only lead to trouble.

Recovering people call it "putting down stakes" when they tell others about their vulnerability to alcohol and other drugs. Family members and friends can put down stakes by letting it be known that they won't keep secrets for their loved ones, that they won't hedge the truth.

When there are no more lies to tell, no more excuses to make, and no more explanations to fabricate, the addict or alcoholic and family members find that life becomes simpler. To take off the mask of addiction and to feel like a genuine human being once again is a terrific experience for everyone involved.

All of us rationalize about a lot of things. We all fall short of facing reality. Denial is part of daily life for almost everyone. How could we make it through life if we were totally honest with ourselves and others about everything, all the time? Saying to ourselves that a head cold isn't as bad as it appears to be sometimes helps us to heal. A healthy optimism can give us comfort when the river starts to rise around our tents at the campsite. Assuming that alcoholism can never happen in our family may give us a false sense of security and save us from worry.

However, excessive and persistent optimism can be dangerous. The head cold might turn into pneumonia. The rising water might require us to move our tents to higher ground. And we all have to realize that alcoholism or other drug addiction is a possibility in almost every family.

People usually don't want to admit that someone they care for is in trouble with alcohol and drugs. During the past fifty years, our culture has become, in general, more understanding and compassionate about alcoholism and addiction. However, there is still a great deal of stigma attached to these problems, and it's a very natural thing that we sometimes try to avoid the truth about them. The truth has consequences.

When we tell the truth, family ties and our deepest affections are on the line. It's hard for families to confront their alcoholic or addict with the facts as they see them, knowing that person may do something desperate or may never speak to them again. Jobs and careers and reputations can be at risk when the family quits making excuses and hiding the addict's behavior from the outside world. Maybe the most important thing of all is that the addict or alcoholic's whole view of life is threatened when the truth is out. You really can't know how that will play itself out. However, if we deceive ourselves about alcohol and drug use, especially if abuse and addiction enter the picture, the alternative to honesty can be the prolonging of addictive problems.

DETACHMENT

People who love alcoholics and addicts do best when they learn to practice detachment. Detachment is a difficult thing to describe. It's not a technique based on a theory of some kind. Detachment comes naturally to some people who practice it without even thinking about it. For others, it's a posture that they learn to cultivate over a period of time. Detachment is something that nearly everyone who is willing to make the leap can pick up on. And it's something that some people are just never able to achieve. There's good evidence that practicing detachment can help people to cope successfully day by day with problem drinking, drug abuse, and other chronic family problems, while they work on long-term solutions to their problems.

Detachment allows for a very special form of caring. Maybe this powerful but elusive psychological mode can best be grasped by considering its opposite: worry. People who practice detachment create peace around themselves, and they promote serenity. In other words, they counter anxiety. Their detachment might be best understood, in fact, as an antidote to anxiety. Detachment frees one to provide caring that is unburdened by fretful, controlling, intrusive, critical, and directive worry.

When a couple or a family or a group of work colleagues sense that one of their own is having trouble with alcohol or other drugs, it's typical for someone in the group to respond anxiously. For example: Dad discovers that Mother has hidden vodka in an orange juice container at the back of the fridge. He has worried about her drinking for quite a while. Maybe he'll have to talk to her about it now. There must be some kind of an explanation. Or would that upset her too much? Maybe he'll speak to their doctor. He can't talk to the kids. He can't sleep that night. No matter what the explanation, the fat's in the fire now. This discovery confirms suspicions and creates new drama and tension. He's consumed with anxiety—and, of course, fretful love.

Overdrinking, drug abuse, and other chronic family problems make people anxious—spouses, loved ones, and others in family, work, or social groups. When a potential problem person senses the family's anxiety, he or she will often respond to it with another round of inappropriate alcohol and drug use. This produces more anxiety in the family, and the alcoholic gets drunk again *at* the family—or at the friends and colleagues.

It's like the insistence-resistance of the backseat driver syndrome: when passengers let it be known they're getting anxious about a driver's fast turns, the driver often has an instinctive urge to speed up.

Now, if an alcoholic manages to quit drinking or an addict to quit using, this in itself can help to reduce the level of anxiety in a troubled family. But we don't have to wait for that to happen. Anyone in the family can interrupt the pattern of drinking and reacting by learning about detachment and by practicing it. This is much more easily said than done, no doubt about that. Getting anywhere with detachment may take a lot of guidance, a lot of support, a lot of courage.

FAKE IT TILL YOU MAKE IT

Some people will have more influence than others. For example, a mother in a traditional family might have quite a bit of power. If she can find enough detachment to quit tracking down Dad when he's hiding his bottle in the garage, a pattern is broken. If she can practice detachment by quitting her habit of calling the boss to make excuses for her husband, another pattern is broken. It isn't necessary for everyone to wait until the problem person changes to start breaking the patterns of addiction. Even a very small change in the pattern of reaction, a little step, can break the terrible habit of escalating anxiety.

Children have a natural sense of detachment that allows them to see clearly and speak honestly. Good friends and loved ones will tell it like it is, demonstrating detachment with love. Generally, however, the more sensitive that people are to one another, the less detached they are able to be.

It has been demonstrated over and over again that for male alcoholics, the person with the most clout is the employer. The boss has a certain natural level of detachment—even when the employee is an old and trusted friend—when success of the business is a basic part of their relationship.

So how do you learn how to practice detachment with love? It may take a long time to learn how to do it. And it may take a lot of work. But it can be done. Here are some basic tips about how to get started on the self-improvement that may help you find your way out of the woods:

- Rule number one: realize that you cannot *make* another person quit drinking or using drugs, just as you can't *make* another person love you. Don't get yourself all bent out of shape trying to accomplish something like this.

- Rule number two: quit analyzing the problem person. Instead, turn your lens on yourself. Look at how you keep the pot boiling with uptight reactions to others. Sit down with a pencil and paper and give some careful thought to how you can get yourself toned down a notch—in simple ways, in your daily activities. The more practical you are in your list, the less prone to endless analyzing you'll be.

- Rule number three: train yourself to quit looking for trouble. Instead, practice being thoughtful, compassionate, considerate, and optimistic. A tall order, indeed. Al-Anon calls this "act as if" behavior. And the important idea is to be consistent about this. As old-timers in AA like to say, "Fake it till you make it."

Put these three rules to work in your life, and you'll be practicing the kind of detachment that can help you through the day. Day by day you can then go to work on long-term solutions. You may still have just as much trouble defining detachment—everyone in Al-Anon does—but you'll know that your life is changing.

There's a postscript to add here: learn how to quit taking everything so personally.

That's the gist of what Ben took away from his

first Al-Anon meeting. The great problem solver, the arch-analyst, was told he needed a whole new set of skills to cope with this problem. He felt less certain about his future with Sarah. At the same time, he felt more optimistic, somehow.

Would he and Sarah marry? Would she come home to him? Soon? Suddenly, he realized that those questions weren't the important questions. They were several jumps out in front of the important ones. The situation was both simpler and harder than he had thought when he was driving up from Iowa in the rain. Now, the point wasn't *why* were things the way they were, it was *how* are we going to build a new life for each of us and, maybe, for both of us? Who knows?

CHAPTER FIVE

*When an Older
Family Member
Drinks Too Much*

Sometimes Peter thought that he should have seen this one coming. It fit with everything he knew about his family, once he thought about it. There's a lot of family history on his mind right now. He's flying from Atlanta out to Nevada to visit his aunt Nora for the second time since Christmas. He finds himself trying to figure out how it all happened.

Aunt Nora had always been a great beauty. A golden girl from the Midwest, she led a glamorous life in fashion design and advertising, first in Paris and later in New York. About 1945, she gave up her career and married George. They left New York and headed west in a yellow Cadillac convertible on the trail of the good life, first on the northern California coast and later in Las Vegas. She and

George never had any children. Peter, as her only nephew, had always been like a son to Nora.

Nora and George went to the great restaurants with the beautiful people in San Francisco; they played golf with movie stars in Las Vegas; they were guests on the swankiest yachts in Los Angeles. And somewhere in the middle of it all, Nora began to drink too much. At first it was just now and then, and just a little too much.

In the early years, her drinking was a charming part of her style—like the hundred-dollar bills she always kept in the rolled top of her left silk stocking, like her strawberry blond tomboy haircuts, like her daredevil flying lessons. Then, some years later, the drinking began to be a "drinking problem"—a matter of some concern. Nora was no longer so charming when she was drinking.

By the time she was well into her middle years, she was drunk frequently by evening, and sometimes totally drunk, out of control, and dangerous. There were some embarrassing scenes, some bitter fights, and now and then a serious problem, including arrests for driving while intoxicated.

By the force of her personality, she could usually bluff her way out of troublesome situations. Until the later years, she managed most of the time— through intelligence, pride, and graciousness—to maintain a wonderful kind of dignity, even when she was drunk. She was such an attractive person that everyone always forgave her. George was often at his wits' end, but he was devoted to her. He would bail her out, no matter what. And no matter what, he always forgave her, too.

Peter's mother, Robin, had taught eighth graders in their small North Dakota hometown most of her life. Long a widow, she was retired now. For many years, when Robin's phone rang late at night, she would know who it was. Nora would call her big sister when things were going badly. Usually, Robin would listen with the patience of an indulgent mother. She always managed to work in an old-fashioned homily on the evils of drink. Then she would let Nora know that she loved her, and she would assure her that everything would be all right.

WHEN WORDS WON'T COME

Peter had known all about Nora's drinking problems for most of his forty-five years. He had never spoken directly to Nora about the subject, and he couldn't imagine ever doing that, even though he knew very well that Nora was drinking herself to death.

This was not simple reluctance on his part. Something deep in his very kinship with this wonderful woman told him not to talk about this problem with her. For all of Peter's life, the drinking had been a part of who Nora was. So also had been Nora's great dignity. To address drinking now as a problem would have been to attack Nora's whole identity. And maybe the issue ran even deeper than that for Peter because, to tell the truth, if his mother had had a drinking problem, he couldn't have confronted her either.

The plane is crossing the Mississippi Delta now at 37,000 feet. Peter recalls some advice he once gave his mother when she and Nora were living together in their later years. "Tell her to give up drinking for a week, to find out for herself if she can do it," he said. "If she can't handle that, maybe she really does have a problem. Why don't you call the AA Intergroup out there? Try to find a women's meeting that includes some older people. No, listen, I'll do that research myself and call you back."

Peter did the research. He found some AA numbers for Nora to call, but as far as he knew, nothing ever came of this strategy. At other times over the years, Peter and Robin talked about finding a treatment center for Nora. Nothing came of these talks either. There were even some desperate discussions between them about having Nora committed to a private facility for older adults with emotional problems. They got nowhere with any of these ideas, of course.

After years of more bad times than good ones, Nora and George finally separated in the early 1970s. And then they reconciled. Several years later, they separated again. During a third or a fourth effort to put things together again, they took a cruise to the Far East. It was to be another honeymoon.

Two days out from Sydney, during a force-ten

gale in the Tasman Sea, Nora got drunk, fell against a bulkhead in their stateroom, and injured her back. She had to be detoxified by the ship's doctor, who kept her confined in the ship's sick bay until she could be transferred to a hospital in Sydney. George brought flowers to her at the hospital, said good-bye to her, flew back to Las Vegas, and filed for divorce.

It was that bad; it finally was that bad. He didn't want to leave her. He just couldn't go on with her. He simply didn't know what to do. George saw to it that Nora was financially all right, and he moved to California. The divorce was final on Nora's sixtieth birthday. She drank to that, all by herself, and then she drank some more. She and George never saw each other again.

The divorce was a terrible experience for Nora. She had been drinking heavily for so long that she seemed to be almost suicidal. Nevertheless, she had always counted on the thought that George would never leave her. There were no children and grandchildren for her to care for. There was no career of her own, and she had no other absorbing interests. Too much of Nora's life had always centered around George and the social life they had led together. Now that George was gone, now that he had deserted her, as she put it, she spent time with friends, mostly widows and other divorced women. They played a lot of duplicate bridge.

Nora often cried to herself, quietly, especially in the night, about the fact that she was getting old. She cried because she felt all alone and afraid. She couldn't seem to help feeling sorry for herself. The vodka she drank during these tearful sessions made her even more depressed. Nora was beginning to die now, little by little, day by day. And she knew it.

THE VULNERABILITIES OF AGING

Even for people who are getting along pretty well in life, the later years are very demanding. These years require as much from people as do all the earlier periods of transition—and at a time when energy is more scarce. Older adults must find enough patience and wisdom to accept what happens as their lives are increasingly governed by the state of their health and by outside forces they cannot control.

Just when it looks like they can rest after the labors of a lifetime, older adults need to summon up all the emotional strength and faith they can find to prepare for the great task of dying. It takes courage to live life gracefully in the face of all this uncertainty. This time of life can present many challenging tasks.

Nora was short on personal resources. Her history of drinking too much left her even more vulnerable to these demands than most people are. Her life had been without purpose for a long time. She really had nothing going for herself—until Robin, Peter's mother, came along again.

Several years after she retired, Robin fell and suffered a heart attack. She went to Las Vegas to be with Nora while she rested up from this illness. The two of them got along well, and they decided to stick together. During this time, things began to turn around for Nora. For a while, that is.

Not only did Robin bring Nora companionship, she really had what it takes to handle retirement and old age. She was a great encouragement to her sister. Nora and Robin began to live a comfortable life together in Nora's ranch-style house in an old and quiet residential neighborhood in Las Vegas.

Peter's mother had given a lot of thought to all the problems of aging. She knew that retirement after long-term employment can create an emptiness in people's lives. She had survived the death of her husband. Lessons she learned then helped her later through the transition into retirement. Retirement, the loss of a spouse, and divorce are all similar in some respects. All of them are deaths of a sort.

Robin had prepared well for her later years. She had made a good financial plan for herself. She had interests in her neighborhood and the community, and she was actively involved as a volunteer teaching people how to read. She had a lot of friends. The only thing Robin hadn't planned for was something she really couldn't plan: how to cope with the loneliness of years ahead when still more of her comrades would be gone and when she would become less able to be out and about. Moving out to

Nevada to live with Nora put that problem on hold, at least for the time being.

A PHILOSOPHICAL TIME

Elisabeth Kubler-Ross and others have written about the later years in life not just as a termination of things, something to be dreaded, but as an important final stage in the living of a full life. These can be years when we observe the ways of the world with a certain measure of detachment and compassion, deciding thoughtfully just how we choose to become involved with it all.

During these years, we can make peace with our lives. We have time for reflection on the past, and we can enjoy the benefits of a deeper understanding of life. It's possible to take satisfaction from small accomplishments. We can find meaning in fundamental experiences and take deeper pleasure in a limited range of activities.

Robin was the well-organized and responsible one who did the bookkeeping, supervised their part-time housekeeper and gardener, and took care of the grocery shopping. She was cast in the role of the mother, the good gray presence who kept Nora in line, most of the time. Nora was the charming child who wanted to please the mother but sometimes broke the rules. She didn't want to get caught, but she knew she could count on forgiveness.

While it wasn't entirely satisfactory, this arrangement was fairly workable. For several years, Nora controlled her drinking pretty well, submitting to Robin's rules and regulations. Usually, she would drink only late in the evening, by herself, in her own room after Robin had gone to bed.

However, Nora never did quit drinking altogether. Once in a while, she would revert to playing that mysterious alcoholic game of drinking, pretending to hide it, but carefully managing to let Robin know that she was drinking, while at the same time denying that she was drinking. If you've ever been around a serious drinker, you have seen this game being played.

As the lives of the two sisters became more and more intertwined, maybe Nora began to take Robin for granted. Or maybe she became bored from living without crises. Whatever it was, now and then she reverted to form. The stability and the companionship that Robin brought into Nora's life improved things wonderfully, but the new arrangement wasn't enough to arrest the alcoholism.

Once in a while Nora was drunk at lunchtime, and then she would sleep all through the afternoon. She hid bottles around the house again, as she had when George was with her—half-pints of vodka in her sewing basket, scotch in the garage tool cabinet, bourbon under the fig trees. Robin would find the bottles now and then, and the two of them would quarrel. When they traveled, Nora always kept some little one-shot airline bottles of scotch in

her purse. It didn't take much for her to be drunk
at this point in her career.

Nora was very skillful at avoiding any really serious trouble. Except for her anxiety about being
discovered, the grim routine of hangovers, and the
inevitable lectures from Robin, she was in fact hap-
pier during this time than she had been for years.
Robin and Nora enjoyed an active social life; they
played a lot of bridge together with friends, they
tended their flower garden, and they took trips. Peter visited them at least twice a year, and for several years, they flew to Atlanta to be with him in
the spring.

And then, with no period of ill health to serve as
a warning, on a warm sunny afternoon late in autumn, Robin lay down on her bed for a nap. She
suffered a stroke and died quietly in her sleep.

ANXIETY ESCALATES

Nora cried when Peter left to go back to Atlanta
after Robin's funeral. She tried to persuade him to
move to Las Vegas and stay with her, but the best
he could do was promise to come back often to see
her. It seemed crazy to him that she could imagine
he would pack up his life in Atlanta to move in
with her in Las Vegas. Now, on his way back to see
her for the second time since she had come to Atlanta at Christmas, he sees that her assumptions
are the ones they're both living out after all. Jane,

his fiancée, had even said, acidly, "If you're so obsessed with her, why don't you just go out and live with her?"

Always in the past, Peter's heart had told him that Nora and George and his mother would work things out somehow. But George couldn't help Nora, and now he was gone. His mother's moving to Las Vegas looked like the answer, and now she, too, was gone. Peter realizes he is all that Nora has and that she needs him, just as he's beginning a new life of his own. Christmas with Aunt Nora helped Jane realize all of this, too.

Peter had invited Aunt Nora to Atlanta at Christmas to meet Jane and her parents. Two of his children came down from Virginia, too. Nora spent Christmas Day in her hotel room, too drunk to see the children. She couldn't remember the Christmas Eve dinner party or that she had met Jane's parents. Peter and Jane drove Nora from her hotel to the airport. This time Nora tried to persuade both of them to move to Las Vegas. Jane was appalled.

During the weeks that followed, Peter spent a lot of time on the phone with Nora. He was getting the late-night calls that his mother used to get. Nora loved him and trusted him, so Peter felt he had a persuasive advantage. Far from being an advantage, the connection between them made it harder for them to be honest with each other. Nora knew how to twist Peter's mind, whether she was drunk or sober, and to leave him feeling sympathetic or guilty or both. Jane almost gave up in despair when Peter told her about their conversations.

Nora could see herself only as a victim of circumstances who had been deserted by a thoughtless husband. She stubbornly continued to insist that her life was meaningless. Peter tried to get Nora to see a psychologist, but she wouldn't have it. For one thing, she came from a generation that didn't have much faith in counseling and psychology. For another, she wasn't ready yet to quit drinking.

Not only that, but the more trouble she was in, the more anxious Peter became when he talked to her. And he knew this! Why was it so difficult for him to get through to her, to make any kind of difference? Why couldn't he get her to ask for help? he said to himself after these desperate midnight phone calls.

Then a miracle happened. Nora called Peter from a treatment center in California. It was a center that was designed specially to work with older adults. She was going to be there another three weeks, and would Peter come out to be with her for a few days when she got home? Maybe it was just a matter of hitting bottom, in the old-fashioned AA sense of the term. Whatever had happened, Peter was overjoyed. And, yes, he promised, he would be there for her.

ADDICTED OLDER ADULTS

Old age brings the deaths of family members, of colleagues, and of the networks of friends that provided one with pleasure, with purpose in life, and with security. Often, the loneliness of old age encourages the solitary drinking and drug use that can turn into alcoholism and addiction. The emotional task of facing up to old age and approaching death can be terrifying for people, especially when other losses are occurring at an ever accelerating rate. Suicide among older men is quite high.

The abuse of prescription drugs is a growing problem among older adults who may only be trying to do what the doctor prescribes. Many of them have grown to believe in "miracle medicine"—to rely heavily on physicians and not enough on their own good judgment. If an older person is over-medicated by mistake, the family will sometimes attribute the ensuing changed behavior to senility.

Alcoholic drinking is the refuge that many people find from their personal fears and apprehensions about death. All too often, families will conspire with one another in the belief that someone is too old to change. Or they will sympathize with older adults who are drinking themselves to early death and agree that drinking may be the only pleasure these people have, so why deny them?

Families can also be cruel to older adults with drinking problems. "There's no fool like an old fool" is a saying that illustrates this point. People who have been heavy drinkers for years usually find

that their levels of tolerance for alcohol decrease as
they become older. We tend to be less than forgiv-
ing of this, less than understanding.

There's a sometimes dangerous problem related
to this lack of understanding. Families and health-
care professionals alike may attribute functional
impairment in elders to their drinking and then
fail to provide treatment for their treatable physical problems.

Old age is something that most of us don't want
to think about very carefully. Research literature
on the older adult tends toward documentation of
the psychological and psychosocial problems of
these people, and the viewpoint is usually pretty
pessimistic. A lot has been written about the social
management of the aged in our society, typically
seeing them as a social problem that requires better solutions. There is alarm among economic plan-
ners about the time not far away when the baby
boomers, who once wouldn't trust anyone over age
thirty but who are now approaching middle age, begin applying for Social Security. Recent census information indicates that over ten percent of the
population of the United States, 22 million people,
are sixty-five years old or older.

Indications are that there will be significant increases in this age group in the years ahead. However, the median age in our society is still relatively
young, and yet we are overwhelmed with the
health-care problems of the present. In spite of all
the activity of the American Association of Retired
Persons and other such organizations, it's still hard

for us to give adequate attention to the needs of the growing population of older adults. There's a tendency simply to write off older people who have mental-health problems, including alcohol and drug problems.

Later life amounts to life on a very fast track: a misstep can mean a broken hip; a high level of organizational skill is required for a trip to the grocery store or to the dentist's office; and going out for a picnic can be as adventuresome as a rock-climbing expedition is to younger people. When there is so very little room for error, the older person who is an alcoholic may find this stage of life to be very difficult. If there is a difference between alcohol and drug abuse among older adults and among younger people, it is only in the fact that the game involves much higher stakes during the "golden years."

The diminished physiological adaptability of older adults makes alcohol and drug abuse among them a life-threatening problem that may rapidly overtax their limited physical resources. For these are also the years during which we become increasingly vulnerable to physical and emotional disorders that compound our social limitations. The high adventure of old age, looked at in another way, is a period of increasing torment and stress. Older people face the loss of their health as they become less resistant to certain illnesses. Once flexible and resilient bodies become rigid and brittle, and the risk from accidents and injuries increases.

NO SILVER LINING

Nora had been as lonesome and depressed as ever. She had alienated almost all of the last of her old friends. Game shows and golf tournaments on TV had been her best companions. Her health was very bad, and several doctors had warned her that her drinking could kill her. Peter learned later that the fire department had been called to her house twice to put out fires—one in her bedroom and the other in the living room. The neighbors had been thinking about calling Peter to tell him what was happening.

So, all these factors had finally added up for her, and she had gone to treatment. Peter felt a great sense of relief. Jane rejoiced with him. Together, they booked Peter's flight to Las Vegas.

Nora was not at the airport to meet his plane. Peter caught a cab to the house. As he walked up to the front door, he heard the phone ringing inside. Letting himself in with his own key, he answered the phone and explained that Nora wasn't there.

That was before he realized that she was sprawled out, passed out, in regal splendor in an orange flowered silk dressing gown, cigarette burns in the sleeves, in her reclining lounge chair in front of the giant screen TV—a midmorning game show blazing away. She was breathing heavily.

In the bright morning sunshine, dappled shadows of the fig trees fell across the patio. The aluminum sliding door to the patio was jammed shut, the house filled with stale cigarette smoke, the old air conditioner laboring heavily. Nora's house was a museum of the 1950s, which was the period when Nora was at the top of her form: there was a state-of-the-art sound system for 78 rpm records, a Uher tape recorder with files of reels, designer chairs, couches, and coffee tables, and Danish modern ashtrays, teakwood sculptures, and wall-to-wall carpeting three inches deep. Everything was yellowed by cigarette smoke.

Without waking her, Peter called the treatment center in California. They said Nora had left the program against their advice the day before. She told them she had to be in Las Vegas to meet her nephew. She had signed a release-of-information form, and they had already been trying to reach Peter. They were concerned because her medical condition was not good. Peter sat on the floor beside Nora holding her hand. She sighed, but her eyes didn't open. She was deeply drunk. Peter finally realized that Nora's problems really were more than he could handle.

He called Nora's physician, who it turned out had helped get her into the older adult treatment program. He came right over to the house. First, he tried to talk to Nora. Then he made arrangements for her to be taken by ambulance to the hospital for detox and a physical checkup. He said he would try to have Nora readmitted to the treatment program. He told Peter that if Nora needed care at home, she could contact a private home-nursing service. He gave Peter a couple of numbers to give to her.

Peter visited Nora a number of times while she was being detoxified, a process that is never taken lightly by treatment and medical professionals, regardless of the patient's age. On the third day, she was well enough for them to do some serious talking. She knew that the games they had been playing were all over now. She agreed to return to the treatment program. Tearfully, she said good-bye to Peter from her hospital bed. And she was able to summon up enough of the old pizzazz to become her genuine and gracious self once again. She sent her best wishes to Jane.

A PHILOSOPHY OF RESPECT

During the next few weeks, Peter went to a lot of Al-Anon meetings. The message he began hearing at Al-Anon was something that he knew very well but that he hadn't been able to live by because he was so anxious. This message was that he could love his aunt Nora and care for her and encourage her, but that, finally, he could not make her change her life. Motivation to do that would have to come from Nora herself.

He knew this in a fundamental way, but it was hard to accept. He knew it, but he had been acting as if he had some kind of a heavenly assignment to do more for his family. And that he could save Nora if he just made the right moves. Now he needed reassurance from others, like the people at Al-Anon, that he had done the best he could do, that Nora would have to find her own way.

Peter kept in touch with Nora's counselors at the treatment center. These people explained to him that they were trying to accomplish some basic things in their work with Nora. First, they tried to encourage her to see her drinking as a physical health problem, not as a moral issue. Without frightening her, they explained just how she was complicating all of her physical health problems by her drinking. They were positive in their approach to Nora and sensitive to her feelings. They taught her some new ways to improve the quality of her life, with a better diet and some exercise and stress management techniques, and by working with her doctor.

Second, they encouraged her to communicate with Peter and Jane and Peter's children, and with any remaining friends in Las Vegas. It was important for her to realize the pleasure of sober communication with old friends and relatives, to realize all the possibilities she had to restore old friendships, to improve some that were going on now, and to make some new friends. To have a full life, we need to keep in touch with the living. Nora did realize how isolated she had become.

After a few weeks in the treatment center, she had pictures of her bridge club members on her dressing table. Nora and Jane were making plans for Nora to visit Atlanta in the summer, when the children would be there. It looked as if life was returning to normal for Peter and his troubled family.

He found himself calling Nora now and then just for the pleasure of her conversation. She still didn't want to hear about AA, so Peter let it go. He really was beginning to realize that he couldn't do anything about that. And things were going so well, so why push it?

And third, the treatment program did whatever it could to promote the self-esteem of these older adults. The counselor explained that the goal of older people is to travel gracefully, with dignity and self-respect, toward all the uncertainty that they face. Inspiring hope within these special people is the principal task in working with older alcoholics, helping them realize how important their journey is, encouraging them to place a high value on later life.

The key is to understand and respect people who are facing the challenges of later life. The staff at the treatment center knew that it really is never too late to sober up. They conveyed this belief to their patients. After a couple of months, Nora returned home with a new lease on life. So it seemed.

A FINAL SETBACK

Then came the phone call from Las Vegas. It was Nora's roommate, Emma, from the treatment center calling to say that Nora was in the hospital, in the intensive care unit. Emma lived in Las Vegas, too. The two women had become good friends, and they had stayed in touch after they left treatment. Peter called the airport, and he and Jane began packing his bag. "Is this all she gets for her sobriety?" Peter asked. "It isn't fair," he said. He was back to thinking things were supposed to make sense, that life was something you could negotiate.

At a brief stopover in Phoenix, Peter leaves the plane to make another phone call to the hospital in Las Vegas. The doctor speaks frankly to him. "She's taken a serious turn for the worse," he says. "Circulatory problems. We may have to amputate a leg, and we can't get her to respond. If we must do this before you get here, do we have your approval to proceed with the operation?"

"Can you, dammit, please wait for me to get there? So I can talk to her?"

"No, Peter. I can't promise that!"

Peter can't believe what he is hearing. The word "amputation" just won't register for him. He can't let himself realize Nora in this kind of trouble, can't imagine her having a leg amputated. The word sounds like "execution."

The gaudy neon Nevada sky silhouettes black mountains far away at sunset. Lake Mead is a silver sheet of water under their glide path into Vegas. It's been a very long day, westward through three time zones. Now the plane sweeps down across a vast cityscape on the desert floor. In the long shadows, suburban neighborhoods are as uniform and drab as vast military installations. Peter marches out through the service tunnel and emerges in the carnival splendor of the McCarren

Field terminal—plush purple carpets on the floors and the walls, stars on the ceilings, recorded celeb voices cautioning passengers to stay to the right on the moving walkway. You hear the slot machines before you see them, row upon row of them, grinding away methodically like production lines in a factory.

Peter wheels the car through heavy night traffic to the hospital, leaves it in the drive by the emergency entrance, catches the elevator to the top floor, ICU. It's a battle station, a chaos of green-clad nurses and aides. A night nurse takes him to Nora's bedside, comforts him. Nora is shrouded in white curtains and sheets, tubes and wires draped all around her. Electronic monitors blink. She looks like a small and frail astronaut in a space capsule. On a steel table, there's a bouquet of red roses from Emma, her treatment pal.

Peter has a two-minute talk with a doctor-in-a-hurry about the several high-tech medical options, what they'd like to do and what they must do, and about her living will. The urgency has to do with gangrene. The doctor makes the decision. They will amputate her left leg above her knee. Peter is stunned.

Nora wakes many hours later, troubled and confused. She thinks that the doctor has cut off her hands but says she can still swim. These are her only words on this last troubled night of her life. She halfway sits up, lifts one arm up and over and then the other. She's swimming the Australian crawl toward heaven. Then she lies back again with a sigh. She's going now. Does she smile? She closes her eyes and seems to sleep again. Peter senses that she's not coming back. He waits alone in the empty cafeteria late in the night, drinks bad coffee from the automatic machines. At last the ICU pages him. She's slipping away. Peter holds her hand, talks to her. Does she hear? And then she's dead. Finally, yes, dead.

In the early morning light, Peter drives through the quiet city back to the house. The desert sun is warm. He leaves the front door open, opens the windows. He notices that the garden is full of weeds. He pours a glass of orange juice and sits at the dining room table, feeling Nora's presence, feeling her absence, too.

Finally, he looks into Nora's bedroom. He's aware of her perfume now. He sees the oxygen machine in the corner. An open jewelry box on her dressing table—souvenirs she must have revisited. There are cigarette burns on the bedspread, on the rug, on the bedside table. Clothes are jammed into open closets. Dresser drawers are in disarray. Cartons of tax-free cigarettes from the Indian reservation are stacked on a shelf.

Under the bed there's a half-empty plastic gallon bottle of vodka, and there's a case of them in her closet. It's the kind of liquor bottle they use in commercial bars. Nora really knew how to protect her supply. Peter puts his head in his hands and cries. There's nothing more to do.

* * *

So, why have I told you this story? A story in which the problem person never really sobers up, just dies? A story in which the care giver seems to be left feeling that he has failed. Why this story? Because this, too, is a reality that some families must face.

I know Peter very well. And he has moved on. Nora's story, so woven into the fabric of his own life, has finally become for him another chapter of his family history. He and Jane are married now, and they still live in Atlanta. They never even think of going to Las Vegas for holidays. He tells the story of his aunt Nora now with a great deal of compassion and with understanding, not just for her, but also for himself.

When his mother died, Peter mourned her passing. Robin's death was sudden, but there was an inevitability about it, somehow. He realized later that she had been preparing for her death—and preparing him. She had even talked to him about her own wishes for her funeral and burial. And she had given him some tasks to take care of after her death. He and Robin had reconciled themselves to her dying as well as they could, in the way we all must do, parents and children, if we possibly can. He came to see that he, too, had been preparing for her death.

Nora's death was another matter, and it was much harder for Peter to handle. Over a period of years, he had had to watch her slowly killing herself, drinking herself to death. That was tough, especially tough because Nora kept suggesting, either overtly or subtly, that Peter could save her. If only he would pay more attention to her—by moving out to live with her, for example—she might be able to quit drinking and get well. And it worked. Peter felt that he was responsible for her not getting well, for her not being happy. When Nora died, it really knocked him for a loop. It was Emma, Nora's friend from the treatment program, who helped Peter through the first few days after Nora's death with some straight talk.

Emma reminded Peter that Nora was terrific—when she was sober. She told Peter that the real Nora would not have held him responsible for her. Emma told him about her own history of alcoholism. And she explained to him that she began to experience a new and wonderful peace of mind only after she quit blaming anyone and anything for her problems. Peace of mind came only when she quit feeling like a victim. Peace came when she realized that with the support of others who suffered as she did, she could be responsible for her own sobriety. She said that Nora had known some of this good feeling about herself, that it was too bad that her own past had finally caught up with her.

Emma talked turkey: people do die of alcoholism. They do have accidents. They do commit suicide. They do refuse help and slowly die of the disease of alcoholism. They do get past all our programs and plans for them. This is what a lot of family members and friends have to learn to live with. We don't have to like it, but we do have to accept it. And we have to learn the important difference between liking something and accepting it.

Emma urged Peter to go back to his Al-Anon meetings. He would need Al-Anon more than ever, now that Nora was gone. After all, Al-Anon was for *him*, not her, dead or alive. Most people who cope successfully with addictions find themselves drawn to a spiritual program of some kind—however they define it.

For some, adopting a spiritual program means a return to religion, maybe the one they grew up with, maybe a new one. Others find spiritual meaning through their association with people in groups such as AA and Al-Anon, "God working through others," as they say. Even the pursuit of physical health can become a discipline that amounts to a kind of spiritual practice. It requires faith, hope, and hard work for some people to stay well.

People like Peter realize they must become pilgrims. First, they do the best they can. Beyond that, they seek the faith it takes to accept with grace whatever follows. It's possible, maybe even especially necessary, in desperate cases like Nora's, for the survivors to be open to this idea. Peter may be lucky to have this faith, but he has worked hard for this luck. After all that happened between the two of them through the years, his memories of Nora have become a vital part of his life. He knows now that the point is not that he didn't save Nora; the point is that he is committed to living with what happened, to making peace within himself.

Peter and Emma still keep in touch. Emma is the

success story he wishes Aunt Nora had become. But that wasn't how her story worked out. Peter's job now, and he knows it, is the essentially spiritual work of accepting Nora for all the wonderful things she brought to him during her lifetime—and for the deep despair she rained on him as well.

CHAPTER SIX

---

*High-Tech Drugs
and Family Ties*

In Kansas, in late winter, if you bring slender brown branches from forsythia bushes into the warmth of the house, the buds will burst and flower. The yellow flowers are an early promise of spring, especially welcome during the short dark days when all living things seem to be frozen up permanently. The forsythia come along first, then the dark green sprouts of winter wheat in the fields, and, a little later, a pale green haze that hangs in the willows along the creeks and rivers. These are things you watch for, even while bitter winds still sweep down across the prairie, while snow still lies in the corn rows.

Jenny is a tall, blond woman, handsome in her sweater and jeans, with that look both youthful and wise that characterizes the new women of her baby boom generation. She stands at the kitchen

window looking out across the red mud of the barn-
yard, past the evergreens of the windbreak, across
to the far hedgerow where sparrows and chickadees
swoop and soar erratically, and on to the yellow-
gray pastures beyond. She's watching for her husband, Tom, who has ridden his horse out to do some
fence repairs.

Their old fieldstone farmhouse is near a cotton-
wood grove in a valley with a creek running
through it. The creek is almost dry this time of
year. The rusty windmill sings out in the yard behind the house as it pumps water for the animals.
Nearby there's a cyclone cellar that Jenny also uses
as a root cellar. Spreading out across the rolling
hills to the west where she gazes are the vast
wheat fields and the soybeans and the alfalfa. Behind her in a large vase in their sunny living room,
the yellow forsythia are blossoming.

As she watches for Tom, Jenny's thoughts are
taken up with Jason, their son. He is coming home
next week from a halfway house for alcoholics and
drug addicts near Kansas City. Tom had all his
hopes pinned on Jason—the oldest child, an ath-
lete, a hunter, the one with a level head for business. When he was just a baby, Jason rode on the
tractor in the fields with his dad. They were close
companions all through Jason's childhood.

Because he had such very high hopes for Jason,
because he staked so much on his success, Tom experienced a kind of disappointment that was a
truly terrible thing to see when Jason's troubles
with drugs became evident. It is still a terrible

thing. It's been almost a year now that Jason has been away, first at the treatment center, then in the halfway house. Tom is grateful that Jason has started putting his life together again, but he isn't about to be over the disappointment.

Jenny and Tom have two children. The whole family together has been managing a large wheat operation, 360 acres of land that's been in Tom's family for several generations, plus several hundred acres they lease. Now that the boys have grown up, Tom has cut back on the time he once spent at his desk and in the fields.

Recently, Tom was appointed president of the local bank, so he's starting off on a mid-life career change. While the children were in high school, Jenny renewed her teaching certificate. When they both went away to college, she began teaching again in the local grade school. Before his cocaine problems surfaced, Jason had been taking charge of the business end of the family's farm company. His younger brother, George, is in charge of the operations end of the business.

THE EXPLOSION

Tom and Jenny were confident that everything was going pretty well as they approached middle age. Jason graduated from college and moved to an apartment in town. Before long, he became a full partner with his father in the farm operation. A couple of years later, George graduated from college and moved back into the house. He brought his own new energy and new ideas to the farm.

And then—the explosion! Out of nowhere. In just a little over a year's time, Jason embezzled almost $100,000 from the family business to support his drug habit. It was a big piece of the farm's line of credit at the bank, and no one was the wiser until the notes came due. It happened so fast, the savings from a decade's work burned away in months. The family took out mortgages, kept the problem out of court, and kept Jason out of jail. Jason was beginning to fall apart by this time, both physically and mentally, and he went into treatment without much of a fight.

Now that Jason has completed his rehab program and is leaving the halfway house, will he expect just to come home again? Both Tom and George say they can't pretend that nothing happened. They want Jason at least to begin to repay the family money he took. Jenny thinks everyone should try to put this bad episode to rest and get on with life. She thinks the family should all just be grateful that Jason is okay now. The issue is tearing up the family, creating an ongoing disagreement like nothing they've ever faced before and that they all hate now. But nobody seems to know how to back down and change gears.

Jenny sees Tom now, heading for the house, on the lane down by the hedgerow—her redheaded Flint Hills cowboy, with boots that make him as tall as she is, and the big hat, the whole cowboy bit.

Her heart hurts for him; she can tell by the way he rides the horse that his thoughts are elsewhere, that the horse is just bringing him home. All through their marriage, the two of them have always worked together to solve the serious problems. But she knows they have never been so strongly at odds as they are on this one.

When he has taken the horse into the barn, Tom trudges slowly up the path to the back door. Jenny has made coffee for them. She meets her husband at the door and throws her arms around his neck and says, "Tom, what are we going to do? I can't go on like this, knowing how you feel about Jason, knowing he's coming home soon." Tom responds to her by holding her close, for a moment. Then, almost without thinking, he pushes her away. He just can't find any words to reassure her: his disappointment in Jason is hardening into resentment. Jenny runs into the bedroom sobbing.

THE ALL-AMERICAN FAMILY

Jason's family is an example of the ideal all-American midwestern farm family. The kind of people who were pioneers in the nineteenth century and lived on the prairie in sod houses. People like this brought law and order to the West. They succeeded in industrializing agriculture. They survived the Great Depression, and all the wars and the weathers of a "century of progress." And recently they have made it through the severe economic readjustments of the 1970s and 1980s.

This family represents some of the most basic and solid characteristics of American life. And these are people who have faith in one another. Once upon a time, in Kansas, good people like this might have felt themselves to be safely removed from such exotic perils as illegal drugs. But today, the fact is, if drugs aren't always available in the county seat down the road, all the young people know where to go to find them anyway, within a day.

There's another important point that should be mentioned about this all-American family. At one time, not too many years ago, Jenny and Tom and their two children might have been seen as a typical family in this country. The breadwinner father, the housewife mother, and the kids. No longer so. Far from being typical, they are an unusual family. The experts have different estimates, but most agree that this type of family represents a distinct minority among fewer than one in American families today.

Maybe what this once-typical family model does for us is simply represent a kind of norm against which we can measure our own situations. And the fact that they live on a family farm makes them unusual in still another way. The family farm is rapidly becoming a thing of the past.

WORSE THAN A NATURAL DISASTER

Cocaine hit the family suddenly, like a summer storm roaring down through the yellow light of a still evening. The first indication came with the problems at the bank. When the careful financial house of cards that Jason had built began to collapse, it fell down all at once. Jason's fraud was all based on deception, and when suspicions were finally aroused, there was nothing substantial in the accounts to maintain the deception. Tom and Jenny were both breathless with fear and dismay when a friend at the bank called them in. This was worse than a natural disaster, because there were absolutely no rules about how to cope with it. Neither Tom nor Jenny could believe that Jason had managed to get rid of so much money in such a short time. How could it have happened? Where could so much money have gone?

Jason first used cocaine at the university, during his sophomore year there. It was a good experience, but it was no big deal. He did it again, only occasionally, always socially, in the following year or two. He and George even did cocaine together a couple of times, later on when George came to the university.

In the second semester of his senior year, Jason began using cocaine medicinally: he did it to stay sharp when he was studying; he thought it helped him feel more alert during classes; and he did it alone, in the evening, just to feel better. By the time he graduated, Jason had some good drug con-

nections in Kansas City, and he was already beginning to develop an expensive habit.

ADDICTION ON THE FAST TRACK

Oftentimes, families who are dealing with alcoholism or the abuse of prescription drugs begin to
recognize problems a little bit at a time. During periods of months and years, most families can learn
to live with the abuses of these legal substances,
adjusting to all the family problems, doing the best
they can about the social, legal, and economic problems that come along, and coping one way or another with the health issues that are often
associated with addiction.

A piece of Al-Anon's conventional wisdom is that
the typical family lives with alcoholism for ten or
fifteen years before its members manage to do anything about it. Whether that's statistically accurate
or not, it's obvious that when people use an old-
fashioned legal drug like bourbon or scotch, there is
usually a long trail of many indicators and inci-
dents and accidents that prepare families for what
is happening.

High-tech illegal drugs such as cocaine can create a sudden, alarming situation for families. Cocaine is so highly addictive that people can become
hooked very quickly. Someone who at one time has
no apparent drug problem can quite suddenly have
a very serious addiction.

As recently as ten years ago, cocaine was generally considered to be nonaddictive, an elegant answer to that run-down feeling. It was expensive, exotic, smart, clean—just the right drug for a very mercenary time. Its initial effect is to make people feel alert, quick, aware, and confident to do whatever business they happen to be doing. The cocaine epidemic seems to have run its whole course on fast forward. Now, it's no longer a little-known underground drug that people think is harmless. In only a few years it has become a factor in some of the most serious social problems our nation has ever faced.

People have to be fairly sophisticated to recognize that someone is using cocaine, when that person doesn't want others to know about it. Of course, there are signs and symptoms, but they tend to be of the sort that family members might not recognize, especially if the person they care about is living away from home.

The symptoms are such things as significant changes in sleeping patterns, moodiness, and irritability; lack of appetite and unusual weight loss; and persistent coldlike symptoms. Other signs are unpredictable work performance, an inability to concentrate, sudden impatience with other people, erratic behavior. A later sign is secretiveness and isolation from the family, friends, and colleagues.

Some kind of financial problem usually begins to figure in, one way or another. Serious paranoia is sometimes a late-stage symptom, at a time when things can turn wild and violent. Most of the earlier signs can be disguised for a time. Someone can become a cocaine addict before the people who care are any the wiser.

Finally, cocaine is a very expensive drug; it's a catalyst to addiction on a fast track. On the street as "crack" cocaine, it is distributed in small and inexpensive but also very powerful doses that are widely available and are attractive to the young and the poor. In the powder form that middle-class cocaine addicts tend to use, it is a high-ticket item. And it's not only that: this expensive drug is a very demanding taskmaster. Its effects are enormously appealing, the euphoria it produces is short-lived, and the urge to repeat the cocaine experience is powerful.

BACK TO TOM AND JENNY

So it happened to Tom and Jenny: their perfect son literally bet the whole farm. He's a coke addict, but they can't bring themselves even to think about him that way. And here they are, the two of them, trying to pick up the pieces and get on with their lives. They've begun to recover from the initial shock. They have taken care of all the immediate and practical problems they can handle. What's coming next for them, now that Jason is preparing to leave the treatment center?

Jenny and Tom have always stuck by each other. But this problem is proving to be a severe test for the family. They've always counted on the support and the help and understanding of friends in their community. With this problem, they are afraid and alone, too ashamed to ask for help from friends. Anyway, their friends probably don't know any more than they do about this kind of thing. They feel quite hopeless.

Only a couple of people in the community know about the extent of Jason's embezzlement. There are rumors about it in the town, but the family is so well respected that these rumors haven't turned into scandal. The problem for Tom runs much deeper than financial hardship or social embarrassment. To him it feels as though Jason has violated an expectation of family members, one for another, that's existed through the whole history of his family. Can he ever trust Jason again?

Tom and Jenny have driven to Kansas City to see him several times during the months that he's been away, and usually George has come with them. Jason spent a weekend on the farm last month for what was supposed to be an after-care planning time, but in fact wasn't, because everyone was afraid to talk. Whenever they've been together, Tom has tried to hide his hurt and angry feelings, usually by keeping the conversation light and by being overly optimistic, all of which just seems to make his true feelings more obvious.

Now it has been months since they discovered that Jason was in trouble with drugs. Jenny and Tom still have the perception that their family was stricken suddenly by a single event—a bombshell.

They don't think of it as a process that may have begun years ago, as something they might have anticipated, as something they could explain if they analyzed it a bit. They just were not prepared for this. There was no hint that anything was wrong, no feeling that as Jason went away to the university, he could possibly be going so terribly far away. Both of them idealized him, each in a separate way. Now both of them want to know why he wandered so far away.

WHY DO YOUNG PEOPLE GET HOOKED ON DRUGS?

Why do young people get hooked, even when they come from good homes like Jason's? When they have all the opportunities that middle-class American life has to offer. When they live in the relative security of a middle-western rural community. When they have families that care for them, good friends, and brave companions. When they have bright futures. The reasons are probably very similar to the reasons behind drug and alcohol abuse among homeless and dispossessed people, young and old; similar to the reasons behind addiction among the wealthy and privileged, all across the land. The answer is that there isn't any one straightforward answer.

Depending on the particular circumstances, and on the point of view of the analyst, there are many ways to explain addiction, with a number of contributing factors. Addiction involves an individual's physical makeup, the environment, one's behavior patterns, the influences of family and friends, one's psychological makeup, and other factors as well, no doubt. In other words, some combination of times and places, people and things, fortune and misfortune, the luck of the draw, if you will, are all among the factors that lead to addiction. At the heart of the matter, however, is the hard fact that the only people who become addicted are the ones who drink too much or who abuse drugs.

When it's a young person who becomes addicted, the principal scapegoats in our culture are the parents. We have a strong inclination to blame the parents somehow. Parent-bashing, as a friend of mine calls it, seems to be a growing industry. We blame parents for setting bad examples for children, or for failing to care for them enough, with the right kind and the right amount of love and attention. We blame them for failing to provide their children with enough emotional support—or enough financial support, or for failing to teach them proper values. And so on.

Because we seem inclined to hold parents responsible, it may be just natural that parents themselves are all too willing to accept the blame when children become addicted to drugs and alcohol. In my own clinical experience, this responsibility is typically a burden that mothers accept even more readily than do fathers, though sometimes the roles are reversed.

During the past fifty years, we have gradually extended the period of adolescence—and therefore the period of implied parental responsibility—for an extra ten years or so. We've added a new category to adolescence, in fact. This is the "young adult" who by implication is not yet old enough to assume adult responsibilities. When things go wrong for these older children, too many parents assume that it's they who have failed.

There's another matter that has to do with parenting. We have begun to see that the post–World War II affluence we enjoyed may not be there for our children to enjoy, too. As time goes by, more and more children are unable to afford housing and to strike out on their own. More children return to live with parents. The average age at which young people marry and set up their own households grows closer to thirty. More young people decide to remain single. These conditions encourage parental overinvolvement and feelings of responsibility that tend to remain too tight and last too long. And so parents blame themselves when things work out badly.

WHO WILL BE THE SCAPEGOAT?

Parents have all of this on top of normal feelings of concern for their children. But if parents take the scapegoat role for their child's addiction, the child they love will not take responsibility for himself or herself. This isn't any kind of revelation. Every parent knows it. It's just that it's a hard thing to accept—hard to live with.

Another scapegoat, one that parents themselves often call upon, is the youth culture or the "drug culture." In their despair, when they learn that their children are in trouble with drugs, many people will blame their children's peers, friends, and colleagues. Sometimes, they will extend this blaming to a condemnation of youth in general.

Still another scapegoat is the illegal drug itself, in Jason's case, cocaine. Alcohol is our powerful all-American psychoactive drug. It's something we're accustomed to. We don't usually blame the bartender for drunkenness, and we don't usually blame the drug, alcohol, for alcoholism. Other drugs that we are more or less comfortable with are the minor tranquilizers. For example, since the arrival of Miltown in the late 1950s, we have persuaded ourselves that a sense of emotional well-being is among our basic human rights. The minor tranquilizers are there to provide us with comfort.

We tend to be much more upset about illegal drugs, such as cocaine, than we are about alcohol. There are harsh penalties for the use of the illegal drugs, such as the amphetamines, marijuana, hashish, and heroin, plus LSD and other eccentric spin-offs from the legitimate prescription drugs.

When we find that someone is hooked on an illegal drug, it's easy for some people to attribute the addiction to the evil hypnotic power of the drug.

Especially if the addict is someone we care about. Illegal drugs inspire in us a great deal of fear and dismay. We have all heard about how powerfully addictive cocaine is. Upset parents need to remind themselves that addiction is not about drugs; it's about people who use drugs.

STAGES OF ABSTINENCE

Jason has now spent almost six months in a rehab program, first in a treatment center and then in a halfway house. And he seems to be doing well. He was sick with despair and anxiety when the family delivered him at the treatment center. The medical staff there monitored him carefully and gave him the medications he required to make it through the first stages of his abstinence from cocaine. It is typical, say the experts, that people like Jason who have become truly dependent on cocaine will experience two or three days of depression, irritability, anxiety, confusion, and insomnia during their initial period of withdrawal.

Typically, then, they enter a second stage during which they may feel very depressed. They may have an increased appetite for food at this time and a craving for sleep. Normally, this stage is followed by a period of days in which the addict feels good, sleeps normally, and has no particular desire for cocaine. This period of calm is usually followed then, unpredictably, by further bouts of depression and anxiety. Often, these periods of mood swing will diminish in severity and frequency over time. This, of course, is not the case for everyone. In many respects, cocaine withdrawal is like withdrawal from alcohol. For some people, sobriety only reveals the deeper problems that still need to be dealt with.

After all this, some people continue to remain very vulnerable to relapse. Just when they begin to feel well and strong again, some recovering people begin to think once again that they can control their use of cocaine. These are the ones who fail to make it. There are others who just never do look back. They commit themselves one day at a time to staying straight. Maybe this is because they feel so good about getting the "monkey off their backs." Maybe it's because they're so terrified of the life they've escaped from. Who knows, and who can ever know about such things?

THE TREATMENT CENTER

The treatment center is a safe place for people to be during this critical time and for a settling down period afterward—a long period for some people, a shorter one for others. It's a place where people who have been through it all encourage newly sober addicts to commit themselves to change. The example of how counselors, who are recovering people, live their lives demonstrates that sobriety is possible. The treatment center is a place where addicts can practice responsible living just long enough to realize that they, too, can handle it.

In a typical treatment center, after addicts have gone through an acute period of medically supervised withdrawal, they are treated like normal, capable people who are able to make responsible choices. Typically, they are not treated as "problems."

Largely because it is an expectation of treatment centers, addicts in treatment soon realize they are capable of living responsible lives. They learn from listening to the stories of other recovering people who are "working the program." They share experience, strength, and hope with one another. They practice responsible behavior in their peer-group living quarters. And they begin their search for peace of mind through attending to humble daily disciplines. These ideas are important aspects of a rehab program.

Most people find it difficult to listen to good advice, especially when it comes to health care. How many of us do what our own doctors tell us? The typical treatment-center method of using recovering people as counselors and letting them tell their own stories of recovery is one technique that works well. The personal stories of people who have been there and now have come back can make a powerful impact. They don't promote insistence-resistance by telling audiences what to do.

Treatment centers provide settings for the kind of personal reflection that allows egos to take a rest. But that's only half the story. Participating in a treatment program means being involved in fellowship with others. A central idea that derives from AA holds that when people gather together to share a common problem, all of them receive at least as much as they give.

A simple thing like making one's bed is a daily exercise that encourages simplicity, sanity, and sobriety through performing a humble task. I know a family psychotherapist who, when he returns from the office in the evening, takes out the garbage to remind himself that he's just an ordinary person, a family member and not a therapist, when he is at home. Making the bed every day is the same kind of Zenlike activity—a small daily discipline that helps everyone feel human.

WHAT JASON HAS LEARNED

Jason has been learning a lot in treatment and at the halfway house about how to take care of himself and begin a new life as a recovering addict. He has spent long hours talking to his peers and to counselors about his plans for the near future.

Jason knows quite a bit now about how his family is feeling, because they all stay in close touch with one another. Because, when he cleaned up, he learned to listen to them. And because he came to know how much he loved his family. He had some trouble figuring out what he needed to place first in order to maintain his abstinence. He tried to figure out how to meet his obligations to his family. How was he going to fit these two things together? Jason really worried about his dad, about the serious disappointment he had brought him. He didn't know yet how he could deal with the situation, but he had some ideas.

One thing he learned was not to act impulsively—to take it easy. But, he told himself, he'd been taking it easy for months. Now it was time to act. Wasn't it? It was hard for him to wait.

Jason has stayed straight for almost a year. With his peers at the halfway house, he lets himself feel good about that fact. His abstinence is the most important thing in his life right now. At the same time, he knows that the rest of the world sees being drug-free as nothing special, as a basic expectation. He has learned never to take his abstinence for granted, but he does feel confident about today. He knows that he can stay clean—one day at a time.

His halfway-house experience has been good: he has learned about the signals to watch for that tell him he's heading for trouble. And he knows where to find supportive friends whenever he needs them, wherever he goes. But when his family comes to visit him, none of this seems like much of an accomplishment, and he feels defeated, foolish, not such a hero to himself after all. They really don't get it. But then, how could they?

THE REST OF JASON'S FAMILY

What about the rest of Jason's family? They haven't been attending Al-Anon, as the treatment center counselor advised them to. They haven't sought out any formal family counseling. They have talked to the pastor at their church, and he has given them comfort and help, but he hasn't tried to give the family any specific practical advice. Aside from this, they have been keeping their own counsel—worrying about what to do after Jason leaves the halfway house, wondering what to hope for. They are still divided on what terms Jason should meet in order to return to the family business.

There are thousands of people like Jenny and Tom all around the country today. Many of them are single parents, dealing with other relationship problems as well as with the problem of addiction. For many families, addiction treatment represents one problem that's being solved amidst many serious family problems that are ongoing. Jenny and Tom are lucky that they are still together, in spite of the strain that this situation has placed on their relationship. They're lucky that working things out, one way or another, is an important family value that they all share. They are lucky that health problems and financial and legal matters are not overwhelming them as they try to make reasonable plans for the future.

THE PRODIGAL SON

It's interesting that here, at the end of the twentieth century, Jason and his family are really living one of the oldest stories in our culture, the story of the Prodigal Son. They're living a timeless problem.

You will recall that this parable is the story of a man with two sons. The younger one took his inheritance, went to a far country, and wasted it all in debauchery, drinking, and gambling. When he was starving, he repented and asked his father to take him in again. The father welcomed his lost son and celebrated his return with a great feast. The older son, who had served his father faithfully all this time, was angry and jealous. The father said to him, "Son, thou art ever with me, and all that I have is thine. It was meet that we should make merry and be glad: for this thy brother was dead, and is alive again; and was lost, and is found." (Luke 15:11–32)

Strange that this famous parable is named for the "problem person" in the story, but it's really a tale about *family* dynamics. The story is told from the point of view of the Prodigal Son—until he reforms. Then the point of view shifts, and it's told from the view of the rest of the family and how they react to the wretched son's repentance and his return to the fold. As the family therapist Murray Bowen might have said, this is the story about a family system.

And who is the Prodigal Son to us? Certainly, these "prodigals" we're talking about are much more than "problem persons." They are citizens to be reckoned with. In fact, they are among the *dramatis personae* of families. They're our brothers and sisters, our mothers and fathers, our own families.

The reaction of the father in the parable is an example of love that never wavers. It is never clear whether or not the faithful son, angry at his bad-boy little brother's hero's return, comes to join the party that the father throws. We're left guessing about that one. Maybe his jealousy festered into a resentment. Maybe he never spoke to his brother again. Who knows? Jason and George face that question. Except Jason is putting a spin on the parable.

Jason *is* like the Prodigal Son—up until his repentance, his rebirth, his treatment. But then, instead of asking to be taken home again, Jason has decided that he needs time, and that he needs to give his family time, for wounds to heal. He has told them he's moving out to Denver and won't try to return to the family business on the farm. Not now at least.

His treatment program taught him patience and the value of time—time for reflection, time for healing, time for reconciliation. It's like the time that's required for a body to mend after a heart attack. Jason was wise enough now to recognize that the whole family needed this.

THE RESULT OF JASON'S DECISION

Jason must have been right. Everyone seemed relieved at the prospect of having some time to rest. The last we heard, Jason was in Denver, working in a music store, attending beginning courses in philosophy at the University of Denver. He hopes to enter the graduate school there—in the philosophy department.

His brother George took over Jason's duties on the farm. A year later, when he married, Jason was his best man at the wedding. George and his wife have built a house near the farm. Whenever Jason is back for a visit, George assures him that his old job is there for him whenever he wants it.

Tom and Jenny breathe easier, too. It was hard for both of them at first. If their own prodigal son was going to reform himself, couldn't he at least come home? Tom is still not over his disappointment, but he works at it. He isn't a man to carry a grudge. It isn't quite right that his first son is going to be a philosopher, but he'll learn how to get used to it. George is doing a good job of filling in for Jason. To tell the truth, he's a good farm manager.

Jenny would have been happy if Jason had married and stayed on to live near them. Secretly, she thinks he may have discovered himself in the traumatic events of the past year or two, and she's grateful for that.

The two of them finally did find an Al-Anon group twenty miles away, in the county seat, and they attend meetings regularly once a week. Their church was a great help to them during their time of need, but they decided they needed something more as well—a meeting of people who were brought together by the issue of addictions. Al-Anon has proved itself to be a lifesaver for them. And now they are able to talk to other neighbors and friends who have encountered drug and alcohol problems in their families. There are a lot of them, it turns out.

WARTS AND ALL

People who learn to carry on and to do well in life, in spite of having to cope with someone's addiction, consistently report two things: first, they turn their attention away from whoever has been seen as the problem person; and second, they put their energies into getting their own act together, no matter what happens in the life of that other person they care about. When they quit taking care of the problem person, they are free to care about this person.

They learn to accept themselves fully, warts and all, in a lighthearted way. They see to it that their lives have purpose. They discover the ability to influence their own futures. They establish a system of basic life principles that helps them keep their lives on course. To sum this up, people who survive the problems of living with addiction are people who have the energy to direct their lives. They are not victims.

They don't just react to others, waiting for others to tell them how to feel. They respect the interests of other people and respond to them appropriately. They can be present for loved ones without becoming overloaded with feelings of responsibility for others. They can love others while respecting the distance between them.

They work hard to maintain what therapists call functional momentum. This is the ability to get things done, within their own limitations. They consistently put a good effort into whatever challenges they face. Others know they can count on them. Energy and dependability are essential in good family relationships.

The prodigal sons and daughters, the people they love, and all the people who love them, too: that accounts for a pretty good share of everyone who lives in this country, doesn't it? Drug and alcohol addiction are such thoroughly human problems, and they are so widespread in this country, that they serve as a kind of national rite of passage, a challenge for millions of our families. If you can make it through this one, as the family in the parable did, one way or another, you've really got something going for yourself.

Suggested Reading

Anderson, Daniel. *Living with a Chronic Illness.*
Center City, Minn.: Hazelden Educational Materials, 1986.

Bowen, Murray, M.D. *Family Therapy in Clinical Practice.* New York: Jason Aronson, 1978.

Carter, Elizabeth A., and Monica McGoldrick, eds. *The Family Life Cycle: A Framework for Family Therapy.* New York: Gardner Press, 1980.

Gallant, Donald M., M.D. *Alcoholism: A Guide to Diagnosis, Intervention, and Treatment.* New York: W. W. Norton, 1987.

Ingleby, David, ed. *Critical Psychiatry: The Politics of Mental Health.* New York: Pantheon Books, 1980.

Jackson, Joan K., Ph.D. *The Adjustment of the Family to the Crisis of Alcoholism.* Center of Alcohol Studies, Pamphlet Series, Rutgers: State University of New Jersey, 1989.

Kellermann, Joseph. *A Merry-Go-Round Named*

Denial. Center City, Minn.: Hazelden Educational Materials, 1975.

Kerr, Michael, M.D., and Murray Bowen, M.D. *Family Evaluation: An Approach Based on Bowen Theory*. New York: W. W. Norton, 1988.

Rice, Dorothy P., et al. *The Economic Costs of Alcohol and Drug Abuse and Mental Illness*. U.S. Department of Health and Human Services; Public Health Service; Alcohol, Drug Abuse, and Mental Health Administration. DHHS publ. no. [ADM] 90-1694. Rockville, Md, 1990.

Steinglass, Peter, M.D., et al. *The Alcoholic Family*. New York: Basic Books, 1987.

Vaillant, George E., M.D. *The Natural History of Alcoholism: Causes, Patterns, and Paths to Recovery*. Cambridge, Mass.: Harvard University Press, 1983.

Walsh, Froma, ed. *Normal Family Processes*. New York: Guilford Press, 1982.

About the Author

Terence Williams has two decades of experience as a family therapist, and is the founder of the Hazelden Family Program. "I WON'T WAIT UP TONIGHT" is his first book. He currently lives in St. Paul, Minnesota.

✳
"EASY DOES IT, BUT DO IT"
with Hazelden Books

THE 12 STEPS TO HAPPINESS *by Joe Klaas* $4.95

BARRIERS TO INTIMACY: For People Torn by Addiction and Compulsive Behavior *by Gayle Rosellini and Mark Worden* $4.95

BACK FROM BETRAYAL: Recovering from His Affairs *by Jennifer P. Schneider, M.D.* $4.95

CREATING CHOICES: How Adult Children Can Turn Today's Dreams into Tomorrow's Reality *by Sheila Bayle-Lissick and Elise Marquam Jahns* $4.99

TALK, TRUST, AND FEEL: Keeping Codependency out of Your Life *by Melody Beattie et al.* $4.99

MEN'S WORK: How to Stop the Violence That Tears Our Lives Apart *by Paul Kivel* $5.99

FROM ANGER TO FORGIVENESS *by Earnie Larsen with Carol Larsen Hegarty* $4.99

"I WON'T WAIT UP TONIGHT": What to Do to Take Care of Yourself When You're Living with an Alcoholic or an Addict *by Terence Williams* $4.99

GRATITUDE: Affirming the Good Things in Life (Hardcover Gift Book and 52 Gratitude Cards) *by Melody Beattie* $16.00

CHANGE IS A CHOICE (Hardcover Gift Book and 52 Change Cards) *by Earnie Larsen* $16.00

Prices and order numbers subject to change without notice. Valid in U.S. only.

For information about the Hazelden Foundation, its books, and its treatment and professional services call 1-800-328-9000. Outside U.S. call (612) 257-4010.